Mindful Magic for The Work Witch

INTEGRATING WITCHCRAFT AND SELF-CARE IN THE PROFESSIONAL REALM

KELSEY PEARCE

KPPD PUBLISHING

Contents

Introduction

MINDFUL MAGIC FOR THE WORK WITCH

W orkplaces can be a source of fulfilment and a breeding ground for stress. Whether you're pitching ideas, meeting deadlines, or navigating office politics, the modern work environment demands balance, focus, and resilience. As witches or individuals who value intention and mindfulness, we have tools to thrive—not by fighting against the current, but by flowing with it, incorporating our craft into the rhythm of our professional lives.

Welcome to the "Work Witch" world, where the realms of self-care, magic, and professional success intertwine. In this book, you'll discover how to infuse your work life with rituals, tools, and practices that ground you, empower you, and create meaningful results—without the need to proclaim your magical inclinations from the top of your office building.

What Is a "Work Witch"?

A "Work Witch" blends intention, self-care, and magic into their professional life. This concept isn't about performing elaborate rituals at your desk or attending a meeting with a wand (though if that's your vibe, embrace it!). Instead, it's about infusing your work with mindful practices that align with your energy, values, and goals.

Magic in the workplace isn't out of place—it already exists in subtle ways. Think of the coworker who won't enter a meeting without their lucky pen, the sports star with a pre-game ritual, or the speaker who touches their amulet for confidence before stepping on stage. These are minor acts of intention-setting, no different from the foundational principles of witchcraft.

As a Work Witch, you take those habits one step further by understanding their energy, refining their focus, and aligning them with your intentions. You can transform the mundane into the magical through tools like crystals, journaling, mindfulness, and rituals.

Why Self-Care Matters in the Workplace?

In a world where hustle culture often glorifies overwork, self-care is an act of rebellion—and survival. Caring for yourself in the workplace is not a luxury, but a necessity. Without proper grounding, burnout becomes a real risk, diminishing your ability to succeed, let alone thrive.

Self-care in a work context goes beyond taking a spa day (though those are great, too). It's about creating a system that supports your well-being amidst the demands of professional life. For the Work Witch, this includes:

- Daily grounding rituals to start your day with focus.

- Energy-clearing techniques to release negativity after stressful meetings.

- Intention-setting practices to align your tasks with your broader goals.

- Tools and talismans that offer comfort, focus, or confidence.

When you nurture your well-being, you enhance your productivity, creativity, and resilience. Weaving magic into your work-life routine lets you stay centred and intentional, even when challenges arise.

It's Already Here: The Magic in Everyday Work Practices

You might not call it magic, but elements of intention-setting and ritual are already ingrained in workplace culture. Many people rely on habits and tools that act as unspoken talismans or charms:

- The lucky tie worn to every job interview.

- The playlist that sparks creativity for brainstorming sessions.

- The desk plant that feels like a silent partner in productivity.

These rituals are a testament to the human instinct to imbue objects, actions, and spaces with meaning and energy. As a Work Witch, you'll learn how to craft these practices to maximize their impact, turning simple actions into intentional magic.

What You'll Discover in This Book

This book will guide you through practical ways to embrace your inner Work Witch, no matter your job or workplace environment. Each chapter will explore tools, rituals, and techniques to integrate mindful magic into your career. Here's a glimpse of what's ahead:

- Personal Rituals for Professional Success: Grounding yourself, enhancing focus, and staying motivated.

- Tools of the Trade: Using crystals, colours, and symbols to align with your goals.

- Navigating Workplace Dynamics: Energy-clearing techniques and protection spells for difficult situations.

- Manifesting Career Goals: Leveraging feedback as a mosaic of growth. Infusing magic into a SWOT analysis for a deeper connection.

A Quiet Revolution

This isn't about waving a wand or wearing a pointy hat in the office. The Work Witch approach is subtle, adaptable, and personal. It's about reclaiming agency in your work life, fostering growth, and staying aligned with your core self.

Whether you're a seasoned witch or seeking more balance and empowerment in your career, this book is your guide to transforming the workplace into a space of magic and intention. After all, your craft doesn't stop when you clock in—it evolves, adapts, and empowers you to shine.

So, grab your journal, light a candle (or set a mental intention), and let's get to work—witchy style.

Chapter 1

ETHICS AND INCLUSIVITY IN WITCHCRAFT

As we bring our practices into daily life, it's essential to approach witchcraft with an open, ethical mindset, especially in shared spaces like the workplace. Whether setting intentions, conducting rituals, or practicing mindfulness, a thoughtful and inclusive approach ensures we uplift ourselves and those around us. Here's a guide to embracing witchcraft with reverence, empowering everyone.

Respect for Beliefs

Like any belief, witchcraft exists within a larger tapestry of diverse perspectives. Not everyone will share the same spiritual outlook, and that diversity enriches the environment. Respect for others' beliefs and boundaries is essential.

Acknowledge the Diversity of Beliefs: Embrace that your colleagues may come from a wide range of spiritual backgrounds or not engage in spiritual practices. This respect can deepen understanding and create a more harmonious environment.

Seek Consent Before Involving Others: While involving a co-worker in a good luck spell or ritual may seem fun or harmless, always ask first. Even positive intentions need mutual respect. A quick conversation can ensure everyone's comfort and foster a positive interaction.

Intentions and Outcomes

In witchcraft, intentions are everything. Focusing on positivity, well-being, and harmony can help create a supportive environment without disrupting the workplace.

Focus on Positive Intentions: Set uplifting intentions and aim for practices that foster collaboration, kindness, and growth. Think of intentions as planting positive seeds that lead to a fruitful harvest for all.

Consider the Impact: Sometimes, our energy can ripple beyond ourselves, affecting the people and environment around us. Before beginning any ritual or setting an intention in a shared space, consider how it might be received. Aim to be a positive force in your surroundings, offering support rather than imposing energy.

Transparency and Openness

Transparency goes a long way in an environment where everyone might not understand witchcraft. If someone is interested in your practices, sharing insights can demystify them and encourage curiosity rather than hesitation.

Communicate with Interested Colleagues: Share respectfully and light-heartedly if a coworker shows interest in your practices. This kind of open dialogue can transform misunderstandings into meaningful exchanges.

Avoid Secretive Practices: Trust is essential in shared spaces, and secretive practices can sometimes create barriers. If your work rituals involve anything public—like burning incense or using crystals—be mindful of others. A quick explanation can make your practices more relatable and foster a feeling of inclusivity. *Adjust your rituals to be inward-focused if you don't want to explain it or fear retaliation.*

Cultural Sensitivity

Modern witchcraft draws on countless cultures, each with its practices and symbols. Understanding these roots helps us avoid cultural appropriation and instead use respectful, inclusive practices honouring diverse origins.

Understand Cultural Origins: Learning about the cultural significance of various practices and symbols is essential. Before incorporating any element from another culture, take the time to understand its meaning. For instance, smudging practices have deep, sacred roots in Indigenous cultures and should be approached with understanding.

Create Inclusive Practices: Consider ways to practice that are inclusive and accessible to everyone. Instead of a culturally specific ritual, try grounding techniques or setting intentions anyone can join in or appreciate.

Professional Boundaries

While it's meaningful to integrate witchcraft into your daily routine, it's also important to balance these practices with the expectations of a professional environment.

Maintain Professionalism: Practices should be subtle and respectful of the workspace. For example, if you like to use essential oils for focus, opt for a mild scent and be considerate of coworkers with sensitivities.

Abide by the Office Rules: If your company has a zero-scent policy, don't bring in lavender sachets; instead, use a picture of lavender as a representation for you to build intention around. Don't bring fire candles into an office situation. If your company has behaviour expectations, ensure that you comply with the rules.

Balance Beliefs with Workplace Expectations: Maintaining professionalism means that your spiritual practices shouldn't interfere with work duties or become distracting. Ensure that any rituals or practices you bring to the workspace integrate into the broader office culture.

Self-Care and Balance

Witchcraft enriches your life, not depletes it. Maintaining a balance between your practices and responsibilities in a work environment is crucial for avoiding burnout.

Support Well-Being: Small rituals, like taking mindful breaks or setting a daily intention, can help you feel grounded without overextending yourself. If stressed, choose a simple, soothing practice rather than an intensive ritual.

Establish Healthy Boundaries: It's easy to bring work home and vice versa, but creating boundaries is essential for your well-being. Dedicate time outside of work to explore and deepen your practice without workplace concerns intruding.

Accountability

Self-reflection and feedback can guide you in maintaining a respectful, impactful approach to witchcraft, especially if you share your practices with others.

Reflect Regularly: Assess how your practices affect yourself and those around you. Are you making a difference? Are you respecting boundaries? This reflection ensures your approach stays aligned with your values and the needs of your environment.

Seek Feedback: If you're open about your practices, ask colleagues how they feel. Open-minded feedback helps you grow and refine your approach while ensuring your practices embody inclusivity.

Avoiding Manipulation

Finally, witchcraft is about empowerment, not control. Focus on using your practices to foster growth and well-being for yourself and others.

Empowerment Over Control: Approach witchcraft with a focus on personal empowerment and strength rather than manipulation or influence over others. Encourage practices that foster mutual respect and individuality.

Encourage Personal Agency: Witchcraft can inspire those around you but encourage others to find their own paths rather than imposing yours. Your practices should enhance, not dictate, the energy in the workplace.

When we bring witchcraft to the workplace, we can be positive, inclusive, and respectful. Practicing ethics and empathy creates an environment where witchcraft contributes to a sense of well-being, community, and balance. Remember: the true magic lies in meaningfully connecting with ourselves and others.

Chapter 2

THE RULE OF THREE AND ITS IMPORTANCE FOR A WITCH AT WORK

The "Rule of Three" is central to many forms of witchcraft and pagan practice. It states that whatever energy or actions you put into the world will return to you threefold—positive or negative. This belief, sometimes called the "Threefold Law," emphasizes mindfulness and responsibility in magical practice and daily life.

The Rule of Three serves as a grounding principle in a workplace setting where energy and intentions can impact professional relationships, decisions, and personal growth. For the Witch-at-Work, it reminds us to approach all actions, thoughts, and spells with positive intent and ethical awareness.

What Is the Rule of Three?

The Rule of Three is the idea that the energy you send out—thoughts, words, or deeds—will be returned to you multiplied by three. This is often interpreted as a karmic cycle, where you are rewarded for positive actions and held accountable for negative ones. The principle serves as both guidance and caution, encouraging witches to consider the impact of their actions.

The Rule of Three can be broken down into these key aspects:

Intention Matters: The energy behind good or harmful actions shapes their outcomes.

Amplification: Energy returns magnified, so small acts of kindness or harm can have larger effects.

Reflection and Responsibility: It emphasizes self-awareness and accountability in all things.

This rule underscores the importance of setting clear, positive intentions in every interaction and decision for a witch, especially in a professional environment.

Applying the Rule of Three in the Workplace

Applying the Rule of Three at work helps a witch navigate professional challenges with integrity and mindfulness. It encourages ethical behaviour, fosters goodwill, and promotes a balanced approach to success.

Setting Positive Intentions in Projects and Interactions

When starting a new project or meeting, set positive intentions. This could mean entering a meeting with openness, committing to make meaningful contributions, or genuinely supporting colleagues.

Example: Instead of tackling a project in a competitive manner, you might focus on collaboration, offering encouragement and help to team members. The positive energy invested will likely be returned through a smoother project flow and a more supportive team environment.

Practicing Mindfulness in Conflict Resolution

Conflict is natural in any workplace, but approaching it with an awareness of the Rule of Three can prevent escalation and preserve professional relationships. Before responding, consider whether your words and actions promote resolution or contribute to negativity.

Example: If a coworker is confrontational, respond calmly and clearly instead of matching their energy. This helps diffuse tension and reinforces a positive, solution-focused approach that can return as mutual respect.

Performing Small Acts of Kindness

Incorporating acts of kindness into your daily routine can make a big difference. The Rule of Three suggests these actions will brighten someone else's day and increase positive energy in your work life.

Examples: Offer help when a coworker is overwhelmed, share useful resources, or show appreciation for a team member's contribution. These gestures can lead to increased support and goodwill from others.

Mindful Spellwork and Intentions at Work

The Rule of Three reminds witches to be cautious about the type of spellwork they bring into the workplace. Workplace spellwork should always be ethically motivated, respecting others' autonomy, and fostering a positive environment.

Protection Spells for Healthy Boundaries

Protective spells can be a helpful way to create personal boundaries and safeguard against negative energy without projecting harm toward others.

Example: Cast a simple spell or create a protective charm to keep your own energy balanced and resilient in a tense office environment. This type of spellwork supports your own well-being without infringing on others, and the positive energy you radiate can help uplift the general atmosphere.

Focus and Productivity Rituals

When casting spells to increase productivity or focus, keep intentions self-focused. A ritual or charm to enhance your own focus and efficiency does not impact anyone else directly, allowing you to work at your best without imposing on others' energies.

Example: Before an important work task, a simple candle spell can invoke focus and clarity. By focusing solely on enhancing your own strengths, you respect the autonomy and energy of others. Unless you are working from home, a battery candle would be the best.

Refrain from Manipulative Spellwork

The Rule of Three strongly cautions against any spellwork meant to control or manipulate others, even if the intent seems harmless. Attempting to influence others' decisions, emotions, or behaviours may backfire, leading to unintended consequences for all parties involved.

Example: Instead of casting a spell to sway a supervisor's opinion, focus on spells that build your own confidence and communication skills, helping you make a natural impression.

Harnessing the Rule of Three for Personal Growth

Beyond ethical considerations, the Rule of Three encourages self-reflection and growth in the workplace. It invites a witch to think about how their actions shape their professional journey and relationships.

Weekly Reflection

Set aside time each week to reflect on how you engaged with others, handled challenges, and contributed to the work environment. Journaling about these experiences can help identify areas where you can apply the Rule of Three more effectively.

Example: Did you offer support to a colleague or keep positive energy even under stress? Reflect on how these actions may benefit you in the future.

Acknowledging and Correcting Mistakes

The Rule of Three also encourages accountability. Mistakes and moments of negativity happen, but taking responsibility and seeking to make amends aligns with the rule's principles.

Example: Clear the air if a misunderstanding leads to tension with a colleague. The respect and trust you rebuild can return to you in mutual support and harmony in the workplace.

Goal Setting with the Rule of Three

Set professional goals with the Rule of Three in mind. Focus on long-term aspirations that benefit your career and support the well-being of others in your workplace. This might mean developing a skill, fostering team unity, or advocating for fair practices.

Example: If you're aiming for a promotion, consider how your growth could positively impact your team. The energy you invest in your development and your commitment to helping others grow will often bring reciprocal support and opportunities.

Embracing the Rule of Three as a Workplace Ethic

Incorporating the Rule of Three at work is about more than avoiding negative consequences—it's a reminder to bring mindfulness, positivity, and integrity into your professional life. By fostering a respectful and positive approach to all aspects of your work, you're setting up an environment where you and your coworkers can thrive.

The Rule of Three encourages the Witch at Work to view each action, thought, and interaction as part of a larger cycle. With each mindful choice, you're contributing to an atmosphere of goodwill and respect that benefits your career and creates a foundation for mutual support and collaboration. Embrace this rule as a compass for ethical, empowered work, and enjoy the growth, balance, and harmony it can bring to your professional journey.

Chapter 3

COMMUTING WITH INTENTION

For many, the commute is a daily ritual that marks the transition between personal and professional life. Though commuting can sometimes feel like a chore, it also provides an opportunity to set intentions, practice mindfulness, and release the day's stresses. By treating your commute as a time for reflection and mental clarity, you can arrive at work more focused and return home with a sense of closure and peace.

Mindful Commuting Techniques

A mindful commute sets a positive tone for the day, helping you shift from home life to work life with purpose. Instead of passively going through the motions, try these intentional practices to make your journey more meaningful.

Practices for Transitioning Mentally and Emotionally from Home to Work

Mornings can be hectic, but the commute offers a precious moment to shift gears and prepare yourself mentally for the day ahead. Simple practices can help you start your workday with calm and focus.

Ideas for a Mindful Transition:

Breathwork on the Move: Use your breath as an anchor. Breathe in for a count of four, hold briefly, and exhale slowly. This will calm the mind and prepare you for the day's tasks.

Body Awareness: Pay attention to how your body feels. Notice any tension in your shoulders, neck, or hands. Release tightness to ease into a relaxed state.

Commute Mantra: Pick a simple mantra or affirmation, such as "I am focused" or "Today, I bring kindness to my work." Repeat it quietly to set a calm, intentional mindset.

Setting Intentions During the Commute

A daily intention gives your mind a focal point, helping you move through the workday with purpose and clarity. Your intention might be a quality you want to embody, like patience or focus, or a specific outcome you hope to achieve.

Intention-Setting Practices:

Visualize the Day Ahead: Imagine a positive and productive day, visualizing yourself handling challenges with confidence and ease. This quick exercise can help you approach your work with optimism.

Choose a Theme for the Day: Select a word that resonates with how you want to feel or what you want to accomplish, such as "clarity," "creativity," or "growth." Let this theme guide your actions and decisions.

Focus on Gratitude: Take a moment to acknowledge one or two things you're grateful for. This could be as simple as feeling thankful for a warm beverage or a productive meeting the day before. Gratitude boosts positivity and brings lightness to your commute.

End-of-Day Reflection on the Commute Home

The return journey is a valuable time to process the events of the day and begin releasing work-related stress. By engaging in a brief reflection and consciously clearing your mind, you can transition more easily back into home life.

Techniques for Processing the Day and Clearing Mental Space

Allowing yourself to review and let go of the day's events on the way home can create a mental boundary between work and personal time. This helps prevent work-related thoughts from spilling over into your evening.

Evening Commuting Practices:

Reflection on Wins and Lessons: Mentally list two or three accomplishments, big or small, to reinforce a sense of progress. Reflect on any lessons learned, approaching challenges with curiosity rather than judgment.

Gratitude Check-In: Consider one positive moment from the day, whether it's a kind word from a colleague or a project milestone reached. Focusing on these bright spots can improve mood and ease tension.

Letting Go Visualization: As you near home, visualize leaving the day's stress behind. Picture yourself setting down any lingering worries or "to-dos" before you walk through the door, so you can re-enter your home life with a refreshed mind.

Commuting with intention can turn an ordinary part of the day into a meaningful transition, helping you step into work with clarity and return home with peace. By incorporating these small yet powerful practices, your commute becomes a tool for mindfulness, intention, and balance—enhancing both your workday and your personal time.

Chapter 4

CREATING A SACRED WORKSPACE

Your workspace, whether at home or in a shared office, can be transformed into a sanctuary that supports focus, creativity, and calm. By bringing intention into your setup, you create an environment that grounds and energizes you, helping you work more effectively while feeling connected to your values. This chapter explores how to personalize your space, even temporary ones, and simple techniques, to cleanse and refresh the surrounding energy.

Personalizing Your Space

Designing a sacred workspace starts with intentional personalization, adding elements that bring meaning, comfort, and positive energy to your day.

Adding Meaningful Personal Items

Incorporating items reflecting your personal beliefs and values can make a workspace more supportive and welcoming. Here are some ideas:

Photos and Mementos: Select one or two photographs or items that make you feel loved or grounded. It could be a photo of a loved one, a souvenir from a memorable trip, or a small trinket with personal significance.

Crystals and Stones: Different stones can offer various energies, such as clear quartz for clarity, amethyst for calm, and citrine for positivity. Arrange a small bowl of stones on your desk, or keep a few in a drawer to hold or look at when you need a mental boost.

Symbolic Objects: You might consider symbols that hold personal or spiritual meaning, such as a small statue, a carved figure, or a piece of jewellery with a special charm. These items can act as touchstones throughout the day, reminding you of your goals and intentions.

Greenery: Adding a small plant can bring vitality to your space. Plants like succulents, pothos, or snake plants are low-maintenance options that thrive indoors and can enhance your focus and well-being.

Creating a Sacred Atmosphere

The atmosphere of your workspace impacts your mindset. Simple adjustments can transform the space into one that nurtures focus and peace.

Lighting: Natural light boosts productivity and mood, but if unavailable, choose a warm desk lamp to create a soft, inviting glow. Adding candles (even battery-powered ones) can also evoke a sense of calm.

Scents and Aromas: Scents can influence your mood and focus, making aromatherapy an effective addition to your workspace. Consider essential oils such as lavender for calm, citrus for energy, and rosemary for clarity. If candles aren't practical, a small diffuser or a few drops of oil on a cotton ball can add a gentle scent to your space.

Sound: Ambient sound or soothing music can help create a bubble of focus, especially in busy or shared work environments. Explore options like instrumental music, nature sounds, or white noise to find what helps you focus best.

Decor Elements: Items like woven textiles, tapestries, or wooden objects can add warmth and comfort. The materials and colours around you impact the space's energy, so choose decor that feels calming or inspiring, like blues and greens for calm, or reds and oranges for energy.

Cleansing Shared and Temporary Workspaces

In shared or temporary spaces, maintaining positive energy can feel challenging. These tips will help you clear and protect your workspace's energy, ensuring it remains comfortable and conducive to your needs.

Techniques for Energy Cleansing Shared Spaces

Everyone who uses shared spaces is influenced by them, so regularly cleansing the area can help you reclaim it as your own, even if only temporarily.

Visualization: Begin your day by visualizing your workspace surrounded by a protective, golden light. Imagine this light as a barrier that keeps negative energies away, leaving the space open to positivity and focus.

Breathwork: Use breathwork to release any stagnant energy. Take three deep breaths, focusing on the feeling of clearing the surrounding space. As you exhale, envision any lingering stress or negativity leaving the space.

Scent-Based Cleansing: Use a small spritz of a cleansing spray (like sage, lavender, water, or vinegar mixture) around your desk area. Avoid potent scents if you're in a shared space, but even a light mist of lavender can refresh and reset the energy. Citrus mixtures also create a refreshing and joyful working environment. Consider lemons, limes, grapefruit, and bergamot diluted in water. When spraying a substance, be aware that it may discolour a surface if not sufficiently diluted. Some mixtures like citrus may discolour in direct sunlight.

Crystals for Clearing Energy: Small crystals like black tourmaline or selenite can help absorb or clear negative energy in a dense busy space. Place one discreetly on your desk to let it absorb any stress or tension from the surrounding area.

Maintaining Positive Energy in Temporary Environments

In spaces that aren't permanently yours, like shared desks or coworking spots, you can still make slight changes that help you feel centred and comfortable.

Personal Rituals: Start your day with a simple ritual, such as arranging your materials or taking a few deep breaths before you begin work. These small acts of grounding can reinforce your personal connection to the space.

Boundary Setting with Objects: Place a meaningful item at your desk, like a small photo or crystal, to define the space as your own for the day. If needed, these small items signal to your mind (and others) that the area is temporarily dedicated to your work.

Mini Cleanse at the End of the Day: Clear your space physically and energetically before you leave. Tidy up your items, wipe down the desk, and, if possible, do a quick visualization to leave the space clear and neutral. Imagine your work energy receding, allowing the area to return to its original state.

Thankfulness Practice: Before you end your day, take a moment to thank the workspace for supporting you. This act of gratitude helps you part from the space with positivity, knowing it has served you well and is ready for its next user.

Creating a sacred workspace doesn't require a private office or a permanent setup. With simple intentional practices, you can infuse any environment with a sense of purpose, focus, and comfort. Personalizing and energetically cleansing your space creates a supportive atmosphere that aligns with your values and empowers your day.

Chapter 5

REMOTE AND FIELD EMPLOYEES

F lexibility is vital in today's work environment, with many of us working from home, out in the field, or on the go. While working remotely or on-site can offer freedom and variety, it also requires mindful practices to stay centred, productive, and connected to a sense of purpose. This chapter explores how to create meaningful rituals and grounding techniques that support focus and well-being, whether logging in from your home office or travelling from place to place.

Home Office Rituals

Working from home can blur the lines between professional and personal life, making it essential to create routines that bring structure, focus, and a sense of sacredness to the day. You can establish clear boundaries through mindful rituals and cultivate an environment that fosters productivity and well-being.

Designing a Sacred Space at Home

Setting up a dedicated work area is a powerful way to fully immerse yourself in your workday, even when you're at home. Small, intentional touches can help distinguish your workspace from your personal space, creating an inviting and professional place.

Tips for Creating Your Space:

Add Meaningful Items: Include personal touches, such as a favourite crystal, plant, or a small talisman that brings peace and positivity to your desk.

Use Calming Scents: Light a candle or use a subtle essential oil blend, like valerian or rosemary, to create an atmosphere that helps you focus.

Incorporate Light and Colour: Natural light and calming colours can boost your mood and productivity, making the space feel bright and energizing. Try a salt lamp if natural light and natural energy cleanser.

Transitioning Rituals to Start and End the Workday

Without a commute, it's easy to feel as though work and home life are constantly blending together. Establishing rituals at the beginning and end of each day can create a sense of closure and help you maintain a healthy work-life balance.

Starting the Day:

Begin with a quick breathing exercise or set an intention to establish focus and clarity for the day.

Engage in a small ritual, like lighting a candle or sipping a specific herbal tea, that signals the start of your work hours.

Ending the Day:

Close your workday with a gratitude reflection, jotting down a few accomplishments or highlights to celebrate progress.

To symbolically "end" your workday, use a physical signal, like closing your laptop or clearing your workspace.

Portable Practices for Field Workers

Establishing a sense of grounding and focus can be challenging for those constantly on the move, working on-site, or out in the field. Portable practices allow you to find moments of mindfulness, even in dynamic environments, to stay centred and connected to your intentions.

On-the-Go Grounding Techniques and Mindful Moments

Being present and grounded in a constantly changing environment requires adaptability. Simple practices can bring moments of calm, helping you stay focused and reduce stress, no matter where you are.

Grounding Techniques:

Breathing Exercise: When you have a moment, close your eyes and take three deep breaths, focusing on the sensation of your feet on the ground. This quick exercise can help you feel calm.

Visualization: Imagine roots extending from your feet into the ground, anchoring you wherever you are. This visualization can create a sense of connection and ease in unfamiliar settings.

Mindful Moments:

Pause Between Tasks: Before starting a new task or arriving at a different site, take a moment to collect yourself. Observe your surroundings or take a deep breath to bring your attention to the present moment.

Touchstone: Carry a small stone or object that you can hold in your hand. Touching it throughout the day can be a gentle reminder to return to a place of calm and presence.

Connecting with Nature and Finding Moments of Stillness On-Site

Fieldwork offers a unique opportunity to connect with the natural world and experience moments of peace, even in the busiest environments. Taking advantage of these moments can replenish your energy and reconnect with a sense of purpose.

Nature Connection Tips:

Take in Your Surroundings: When you're outside, even for a few minutes, appreciate the sights, sounds, and scents around you. Engage with nature by noticing details, like the colour of the sky or the sound of nearby birds.

Practice Earthing: Remove your shoes and let your feet touch the earth. This practice, known as "earthing," can help you feel grounded and rejuvenated.

Finding Stillness:

Silent Reflection: When possible, take a few moments of quiet to check in with yourself. Use this time to release any stress and reconnect with your intentions for the day.

Mini-Meditations: Even a minute or two of meditation can create a sense of calm and focus. Close your eyes and breathe deeply, allowing each breath to relax and re-centre you.

Whether working from a home office or moving between locations, creating a sense of ritual and mindfulness can transform your workday. By tailoring these practices to your unique environment, you'll foster a strong connection to your work, maintain a sense of grounding, and feel more balanced and fulfilled in each day's journey.

Chapter 6

DIVINATION FOR INSIGHT IN THE WORKPLACE

D ivination is often seen as mystical and mysterious, but at its core, it's simply a tool for reflection, helping us explore different perspectives and possibilities. In a workplace setting, divination can serve as a gentle prompt for self-awareness and creative problem-solving. Think of it as a practice for opening your mind, rather than a means to dictate decisions or outcomes.

Purpose of Divination in a Work Setting

Incorporating divination into your work life doesn't mean using tarot cards or runes as strict guides or expecting exact predictions. Instead, divination can be a helpful, meditative tool for personal insight and reflection.

Reflection, Not Dictation: Divination is about gaining perspective rather than being told what to do. If you face a work challenge or need to decide, tools like tarot or witch stones can offer ideas and viewpoints you may not have considered. This approach promotes self-reflection, inviting you to consider possibilities and weigh options with an open mind.

Open-Minded Exploration: Through thoughtful questions, divination encourages open-mindedness and helps you expand your understanding of a situation. For instance, a tarot card might represent "patience" or "perseverance," prompting you to reflect on how these qualities might influence your approach to a project or problem.

Tools and Techniques

You don't need a full altar or complex spreads to bring divination into the workplace—small, practical applications work best in a professional setting. Here's an overview of some accessible tools and how they can gain insight in a work-friendly way.

Tarot Cards

Tarot cards are a versatile and visually engaging tool. A simple one-card or three-card spread is ideal for quick, meaningful reflections.

One-Card Pull: Pull a single card with a question in mind, like "What energy should I bring to this project today?" or "What should I be mindful of in my interactions?" This gives you a concise prompt to consider as you go about your day.

Three-Card Spread: The classic "Past, Present, Future" spread can also be adapted for work. For instance, think of the cards as representing the background of the situation, your current challenge, and potential outcomes based on your approach. This gives you a balanced look at the issue and directions.

> **Tarot Card Example:** We ask the question "What energy should I bring to this project today?" and we pull "The Hierophant". The Hierophant, also known as the High Priest or Pope in some decks, is a card that signifies conformity, established institutions, and spiritual guidance. The hierophant values structure and organization, today may be a day to pre-plan and structure conversations. The hierophant is also a leader so either lean into your own leadership and strengths or seek a mentor if this isn't your strength.

Nordic Runes

Runes are a set of symbols, each with unique meanings, that can be cast or drawn one at a time. They work well when seeking a clear focus or insight on a single aspect.

Single Rune Draw: Much like the one-card tarot pull, a single rune can act as a focus point for the day, helping you think about a particular theme, such as growth, stability, or perseverance.

Three-Rune Draw: Pulling three runes can provide a broader view. You might frame them as "Where am I now?", "What should I focus on?" and "What can I release or change?"

> **Nordic Rune Example:** Perhaps we are reviewing our performance and goal setting. Let's pull three runes, as we pull each stone we focus on the three questions above "Where am I now?", "What should I focus on?", and "What can I release or change?". For the first question we pull Raidho representing journey, movement, and progress. This seems easy to infer we are on a journey, aren't we all? But as we contemplate what Raidho means perhaps you are like me and consider that fear has been holding us back on embracing our journey. After consideration we pull the second rune asking "What should I focus on?". We pull Othala, heritage, home, inheritance. Interpreting Othala we recognize that this is a good time to leverage values from our heritage or developed within our family and friend group. For me, when I pulled Othala, I recognized that my fear from the first pull was directly related to some traits I am fearful of inheriting and what that might mean. Finally, we pull the third rune asking "What can I release or change?", we pull Wunjo, joy, harmony, success. This doesn't mean we release things that cause us joy, rather we could release what isn't bringing us joy, or I could release my fears and try to find harmony.

As you can see, reflecting over several runes can be insightful as it leads you through questions and prompts for self-discovery.

Witch Rune Stones

Like Nordic runes, witch stones are small, portable symbols that often carry specific messages. They can be pulled as guidance or reminders during the day.

Framing Your Question: Before pulling a stone, consider questions that open up possibilities, such as "What am I overlooking?" or "What do I need to be mindful of?" This approach invites you to think critically and explore beyond the immediate task.

Witch Rune Example: we have a deliverable that doesn't feel complete. We grab our pouch of witch runes (the thirteen stone set, there are different types), take a breath in and long breath out either thinking or asking out loud "What am I missing?". We draw the "wave" symbolled stone. As we think about waves and their symbols we consider that waves can move us around without direction, they can hide what is beneath the surface, and maybe we feel adrift. The wave is also linked to our intuition. If that was me, I would first reassure myself that my intuition was correct. If stuck in the waves I might hold the "flight" stone and look for a higher perspective; a little distance, mentally or physically that can provide clarity.

What if You Don't Know How to Interpret Divination Tools?

You are not alone, there is a lot of meaning even differences of opinion. Remember first, it is only to provide insight. You can use images especially with Tarot cards and Witch Runes and infer what the images means to you. If you are new to these tools, I would suggest the Witch Runes since there are fewer stones/cards. Most sets come with simple instructions.

A new source of development is using an AI tool like Co-Pilot or ChatGPT if you feel comfortable. Simply type the question you asked and the card or rune pulled. Much like reading from a book, you take what you want from an AI tool reference.

Integrating Insight into Decision-Making

While divination can be insightful, it should serve as a guide to new perspectives, not a rigid answer. Here's how to use these insights in a balanced, practical way:

Alternative Perspectives: If your divination points toward a quality or outcome, ask yourself, "How might this apply?" or "What other ways could I look at this situation?" For example, a tarot card suggesting "patience" might encourage you to delay sending a hasty email or give a team member extra time on a task. It's about allowing the insight to influence you rather than feeling bound by it.

Reflective Journaling: Consider keeping a small journal to jot down any significant divination insights and how you incorporate them into your day or decisions. Reflect on your feelings about the insight and how it influenced your choices. Over time, you'll start noticing patterns and perhaps gain a deeper understanding of your intuitive responses in the workplace.

Reflection Over Reaction

One of divination's most valuable aspects is its ability to cultivate a reflective mindset. Rather than jumping to conclusions or taking immediate action, you can use divination to pause, assess, and approach work challenges with a sense of calm and clarity.

Exploring Possibilities: See divination as an opportunity to "try on" different perspectives and assess potential actions without commitment. It's like brainstorming but focusing on internal wisdom and creative intuition.

Self-Awareness, Not Prediction: Remember that divination is a tool for exploration rather than a way to predict the future. The insights you gain will enhance your awareness and help you see situations from a broader viewpoint. Instead of expecting a specific outcome, use your reading as a reminder to stay mindful, adaptable, and open to possibilities.

By approaching divination with curiosity and balance, you can integrate it as a practical, insightful practice that complements your professional goals. This mindset allows you to grow in confidence, develop your intuition, and decide with greater thoughtfulness, helping you navigate the workplace with clarity and calm.

Chapter 7

TALISMANS AND SYMBOLS

Talismans and symbols have long been used to invite specific energies, focus intentions, and create meaningful connections with our goals. In the workplace, they can nudge us to remember our intentions or offer silent encouragement as we go about our day. This chapter explores how to craft personal talismans using simple materials and incorporate symbols into your workspace in authentic, yet subtle, ways.

Crafting Personal Talismans

Creating a talisman can be as simple or intricate as you'd like. A personal talisman is unique to you, carrying energy that aligns with your intentions and goals. Here's how to make one from materials you may already have at home.

Choosing Your Materials: Start by thinking about your intention. Is it confidence? Creativity? Protection? Select materials that resonate with these intentions. Common items include stones, small pieces of fabric, beads, and twine. For example:

Stones: Crystals like amethyst, tiger's eye, or clear quartz can be small yet powerful additions to a talisman, each with specific properties.

Fabric and Thread: If you have a favourite colour that evokes strength or calm, use it to wrap or bind your talisman. Colours carry their energies and can help reinforce your intentions.

Personal Items: Add small, meaningful items, like a family heirloom button or a bead from a favourite bracelet.

Creating a Charm or Talisman: Once you have your materials, find a quiet space to work. Set your intention, focusing on what you want the talisman to bring into your life.

Assembly: Tie or wrap your items together, focusing on your intention with each knot or addition.

Infusing Your Intention: When your talisman is complete, hold it in your hands and take a moment to infuse it with your intention. Visualize the energy you want it to carry, whether confidence, peace, or focus.

Keeping It Close: Once finished, you can carry your talisman in a pocket, keep it in a drawer at work, or even tuck it into a small pouch attached to your keychain. It serves as a personal, discreet source of energy you can connect with whenever you need a reminder of your intentions.

Overview of Workplace Symbols and Their Meanings

Certain symbols are used to promote positive energy and focus on workspaces. Here are a few symbols you might incorporate into your talisman or your workspace:

The Spiral: Often represents growth, change, and evolution. It's an excellent symbol if you're seeking to embrace adaptability or expand your skills.

The Triangle: An upward-pointed triangle symbolizes stability, strength, and action, while a downward-facing triangle is often associated with balance and grounding.

The Eye: The "evil eye" symbol is used to ward off negativity. Small charms featuring this symbol can subtly remind you to protect your energy.

Feathers: Represent lightness and clarity. A feather or feather symbol nearby can help you stay connected to a sense of freedom and clear-headedness.

The Infinity Symbol: Often represents interconnectedness and endless possibilities, making it a symbol for those working in creative fields or problem-solving roles.

The Circle: A simple circle can represent wholeness and unity, encouraging harmonious interactions with colleagues or within a team.

Incorporating Symbols into the Workspace

Adding symbols to your workspace doesn't have to be overt. Subtle incorporation can make them feel more personal and less like a "statement," especially in a professional setting. Here are some ideas for integrating symbols that align with your intentions but are still workplace-friendly.

Desk Items and Decor: Consider small decorative pieces like paperweights, coasters, or subtle art prints that feature your chosen symbols. For example, a coaster with a mandala pattern could serve as a visual reminder of focus and unity.

Personal Accessories: If you're concerned about decor in shared spaces, incorporating symbols into accessories is a discreet way to bring intention into your day. Jewellery, like a necklace with an infinity symbol or a bracelet featuring a protective charm, is a subtle and stylish way to carry symbols with you.

Stationery and Supplies: Choose notebooks, pens, or sticky notes that feature designs aligned with your intentions. Small, intentional choices, like a notepad with a grounding tree motif, can add meaning to your everyday tools.

Pinned Items or Mini Altars: If you have a personal desk, consider setting up a mini altar or pinboard with symbolic items. A small dish with stones or a pinned picture of a symbolic image can create a meaningful "sacred" space without taking up too much room. This space can become your go-to spot when you must re-centre or refocus.

Digital Symbols: Digital symbols are a fantastic option for those who work remotely or in tech-heavy spaces. You could use a meaningful symbol as your desktop wallpaper, phone background, or a subtle icon on your taskbar. These images can serve as little touchpoints of intention every time you glance at them.

Doodle Brainstorming: Use symbols when doodling and brainstorming. I draw bowls while I am thinking and envisioning them, capturing my ideas.

Integrating talismans and symbols into your workspace is a beautiful way to enhance your connection to your intentions without drawing undue attention. You can create a space that feels supportive, purposeful, and uniquely yours through thoughtful, subtle choices. Each item, whether a stone in your pocket or a meaningful background on your screen, becomes part of a daily ritual that keeps you connected to the energy and focus you wish to bring to your work. In the next chapter, we will use symbols to create a SWOT.

Chapter 8

THE MAGIC OF SWOT—A PRACTICAL TOOL FOR PLANNING AND REFLECTION

S elf-assessment and performance planning tools in the modern workplace can help clarify goals, identify opportunities, and manage challenges. One such tool, the SWOT analysis, often used in business strategy, yields similar results when applied to one's own life. What makes SWOT especially compelling for work witches is its flexibility—it can be infused with magical intention to become a tool for planning and a means for self-reflection and transformation.

SWOT: A Framework for Insight

The SWOT analysis is a matrix divided into four quadrants:
- Strengths (Internal/Positive)

- Weaknesses (Internal/Negative)

- Opportunities (External/Positive)

- Threats (External/Negative)

This structure provides a comprehensive view of internal and external influences on a situation or goal, balancing positive and negative aspects.

Understanding the Quadrants

Each quadrant has a distinct purpose and energy:

Strengths (Internal/Positive)

What It Is: Strengths represent the skills, resources, and qualities you already possess. These are the foundations on which you can build success.

Magical Perspective: This quadrant resonates with grounding and empowerment. Here, you acknowledge your inner magic—talents, achievements, and personal power.

Questions to Ask:

- What am I naturally good at?

- What resources (skills, relationships, tools) can I rely on?

- How does my magic or intuition support my goals?

Weaknesses (Internal/Negative)

What It Is: Weaknesses are the areas where improvement is needed. These could be gaps in skills, habits, or limiting beliefs that hold you back.

Magical Perspective: Weaknesses are not failures but opportunities for transformation. Use this quadrant to reflect on what you can release or improve.

Questions to Ask:

- What skills or knowledge do I need to develop?

- Where do I feel most vulnerable or unprepared?

- Are there any negative habits or energies I need to address?

Opportunities (External/Positive)

What It Is: Opportunities are external factors you can leverage to your advantage. These might include trends, relationships, or upcoming events that align with your goals.

Magical Perspective: This quadrant reflects the energy of growth and expansion. It's a space to identify opening doors and set intentions to seize them.

Questions to Ask:

- What external opportunities are available to me?

- Are there people or resources that could support my growth?

- How can I align my intentions to attract positive opportunities?

Threats (External/Negative)

What It Is: Threats represent external challenges or obstacles that could hinder your progress. These might be competitors, shifting circumstances, or unforeseen difficulties.

Magical Perspective: Threats call for protection and adaptability. Use this quadrant to identify what you need to shield against and how to stay flexible in facing adversity.

Questions to Ask:

- What external factors could disrupt my plans?

- Are there conflicts or challenges I need to prepare for?

- How can I use protective or grounding magic to stay resilient?

SWOT as a Magical Tool

A SWOT analysis doesn't have to be analytical—it can be a sacred ritual of self-reflection and intention-setting. Here's how to incorporate magic into your

SWOT process. A SWOT table is available at the end of this chapter. Place your crystals and focus on the quadrant.

Preparation:

Choose a quiet space and gather any tools that enhance your focus, such as candles, crystals, or a journal.

Consider aligning your session with the lunar cycle. For example, perform your SWOT during a waxing moon for growth and opportunities, or a waning moon for releasing weaknesses and threats.

Set Your Intentions:

Before you begin, take a few moments to centre yourself. Light a candle or take deep breaths to connect with your intuition.

State your purpose: "I will use this reflection to uncover my strengths, transform my weaknesses, seize my opportunities, and protect against challenges."

Engage with Symbolism:

As you complete each section, visualize the energy of that quadrant. For example, imagine a golden light in the Strengths quadrant or a protective shield in the Threats quadrant. Leverage the SWOT diagram in this book as a starting point for visualizing your analysis.

Infuse Geometric Magic:

Visualize your SWOT diagram as a sacred grid. Assign shapes or symbols to each quadrant that resonate with its energy. For example:

- Strengths: Upward triangle (growth and ambition).

- Weaknesses: Spiral Inward (self-reflection and understanding of deeper issues).

- Opportunities: Circle (cycle and unity).

- Threats: Pentagon and/or zigzags (protection and warding off external influences).

The Quadrants as a Magical Compass

Imagine the SWOT diagram as a magic compass or energy grid, with each quadrant representing a cardinal direction and its associated energies. This visualization helps create a balanced, harmonious flow of energy between the elements of your plan.

Each quadrant can align with a cardinal direction, allowing you to draw on the symbolic power of these directions:

- North (Strengths): Stability, growth, grounding energy. Focuses on what you already possess.

- South (Weaknesses): Transformation, self-awareness, and releasing what no longer serves.

- East (Opportunities): New beginnings, ideas, and potential external growth.

- West (Threats): Reflection, protection, and dealing with external challenges.

You can visualize this as a compass wheel that balances all aspects of your SWOT, helping to align your energy with your external environment.

Crystal Support:

Place a crystal associated with each quadrant near your SWOT chart. An example of a crystal for each quadrant is listed below, but don't limit yourself. Pick from what you have available or what resonates with you:

- Strengths: Citrine (confidence and abundance).

- Weaknesses: Black tourmaline (grounding and transformation).

- Opportunities: Green aventurine (luck and growth).

- Threats: Amethyst (clarity and protection).

A simple, clear quartz moved from quadrant to quadrant, amplifying your ritual as you progress through each quadrant's evaluation.

Create a Ritual Closing:

After completing your SWOT, close with gratitude. Thank your intuition, guides, or the universe for supporting your reflection.

Seal your intentions: "I am aligned with my strengths, open to opportunities, adaptable to challenges, and resilient in all things."

SWOT for Subtle Collaboration

When using SWOT professionally, you can maintain its practical focus while infusing it with your intentions:

- Visualize the magical correspondences in your mind while presenting the chart.

- Subtly place a small object (like a crystal in your pocket) that connects to the quadrant you want to amplify.

- Incorporate positive, empowering language when discussing each quadrant to create an energy of collaboration and possibility.

By embracing SWOT as both a practical and magical tool, you transform performance planning into a journey of self-discovery and empowerment. Each quadrant becomes a portal to greater insight, balancing the external and internal, the positive and negative, to guide you toward success and resilience. Whether used alone or in collaboration, a magical SWOT can help you align your goals with your highest intentions and create a clear path forward.

The Witches SWOT

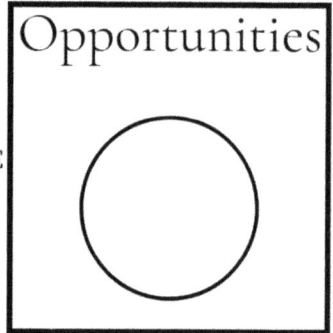

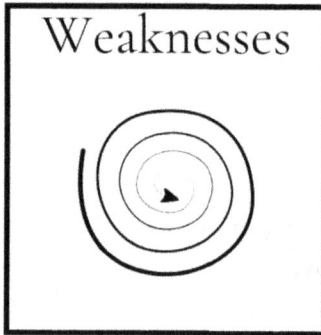

Strengths

Threats

Opportunities

Weaknesses

Chapter 9

THE FEEDBACK JAR: TRANSFORMING INSIGHTS INTO A MOSAIC OF GROWTH

Reframing Feedback as Magic

F eedback is a cornerstone of growth, providing insights that guide our personal and professional journeys. The Feedback Jar is a magical tool for the Work Witch to transform every piece of feedback into a tangible and empowering ritual. Through this practice, feedback becomes a positive force, reinforcing self-awareness, intentionality, and confidence.

The Symbolism of the Feedback Jar

Imagine a clear jar gradually filling with vibrant beads, each one symbolizing a moment of growth, gratitude, or insight. This is more than a simple jar; it's a mosaic that tells the story of your journey.

The jar's transparency reflects a spirit of openness—every piece of feedback contributes to your evolution. Whether it represents an opportunity to refine your skills or a moment of celebration, each bead adds beauty and balance to the whole.

Creating Your Feedback Jar Ritual

What You'll Need:
- A clear jar (glass or acrylic works best for visualization).

- Coloured glass beads, stones, or marbles in different colours.

- A notebook or small cards for reflections, if desired.

- Optional: a sigil or symbol of intention to place at the bottom of the jar.

Assigning Colours to Feedback:

Select colours that resonate with the various types of feedback you receive. For example:

Green: Developmental insights representing growth and learning.

Blue: Positive reinforcement or affirming feedback, symbolizing calm and confidence.

Yellow: Expressions of gratitude, such as thank-you or acknowledgments, for fostering warmth and optimism.

Red: Energizing or thought-provoking feedback, representing passion and motivation.

White: Self-reflection or moments of personal insight.

Optional: Assign a colour to feedback you were unsure how to incorporate, perhaps even disagree with. We accept the given feedback but will not give it the same weight. A clear bead or marble would work to acknowledge it but not allow it to define you.

How to Use the Feedback Jar in Your Daily Life

Receiving Feedback:

When you receive feedback, whether it's formal or informal, take a moment to reflect. Identify the essence of the feedback—is it a celebration of success, a suggestion for refinement, or an appreciation of your contributions? Choose a bead colour that aligns with its nature.

Placing the Bead:

Hold the bead in your hand and set an intention as you prepare to add it to the jar. For example:
- "I embrace this feedback as a tool for growth and evolution."

- "I honour this appreciation and allow it to strengthen my confidence."

Place the bead into the jar, visualizing how it contributes to the growing mosaic of your professional and personal story.

Reflecting on Insights:

For feedback that sparks curiosity or invites improvement, journal or med895+itate on its message. How can it help refine your strengths or reveal new opportunities? Add the bead when you're ready to appreciate its value.

The Power of Visualization: A Holistic Approach to Growth

As the jar fills, it physically represents your dedication to growth and balance. The diversity of colours symbolizes a well-rounded journey, with each insight contributing to your evolution.

Even the beads that represent areas for improvement enhance the beauty of the jar, showing how every experience adds depth and richness to your professional and personal identity.

Infusing Magical Intention

Take your Feedback Jar practice deeper by adding magical elements:

Quarterly Reflection Ritual: Review the jar every three months. Notice which colours are most abundant and reflect on how they align with your goals. Celebrate your progress and set new intentions.

New Year's Magic: Empty the jar at the end of the year and reflect on the mosaic you've created. Place a new intention card or sigil at the bottom of the jar for the upcoming year.

Energetic Cleansing: Regularly cleanse the jar with smoke, sound, or moonlight to keep its energy fresh and vibrant.

Building Your Beautiful Mosaic

The Feedback Jar transforms feedback into an act of magic and mindfulness. By embracing insights with intention, you shift from simply receiving feedback to actively weaving it into a narrative of growth and empowerment.

As the jar fills, it stands as a testament to your resilience, adaptability, and commitment to self-improvement. Each bead, each colour, each moment tells a story—a story of a Work Witch who knows how to turn everyday experiences into a magical mosaic of success.

Chapter 10

MINDFULNESS TECHNIQUES

Mindfulness is the art of staying present and aware, no matter what the day brings. In a work setting, practicing mindfulness can keep you grounded, boost focus, and help manage stress. Whether you're at a desk, on your feet, or out in the field, there are mindfulness techniques that can fit into your day without interrupting your workflow. This chapter introduces quick, practical exercises for both desk workers and field employees, showing how small moments of calm can make a big impact.

Quick Practices for Desk Workers

If you spend a lot of time at a desk, you know how easy it is to get absorbed in tasks and lose track of time. These desk-friendly mindfulness exercises can help you stay centred and reduce stress, no matter how busy the day gets.

Breathing Techniques for Centreing

The simplest and quickest way to regain calm is through controlled breathing. Here are a few techniques you can try while sitting at your desk:

- 4-7-8 Breathing: Inhale for a count of four, hold for seven, and exhale for eight. This method helps slow the heart rate and calm the nervous system, and it is especially useful before a big meeting or when feeling overwhelmed.

- Box Breathing: Inhale for four counts, hold for four, exhale for four, and hold again for four. This steady rhythm helps focus the mind and reset your energy, making it ideal for midday breaks.

Visualization for Calm and Focus

Visualization is a great way to mentally step back, even if you can't physically leave your desk.

Safe Place Visualization: Close your eyes and imagine a calming, safe place—maybe a beach, a peaceful forest, or a cozy room. Spend a few moments visualizing yourself there, breathing in the atmosphere. This simple practice can help reset your mood in under five minutes.

Goal Visualization: If you're preparing for a task or a challenging project, spend a few minutes visualizing yourself conquering it. Imagine the positive emotions of accomplishment, which can help you stay motivated and focused.

Grounding Techniques for Awareness

Grounding exercises bring your attention back to the present, helping you reconnect with your surroundings. This is especially helpful during moments of stress or when you're feeling scattered.

5-4-3-2-1 Technique: Notice five things you can see, four things you can touch, three things you can hear, two things you can smell, and one thing you can taste. This practice anchors you in the present, giving your mind a mini-break from tasks. From personal experience, this is an excellent exercise to practice daily for yourself or with children. In times of high stress, lean on this skill to help mitigate some of the anxiety.

Foot Grounding: Place your feet flat on the floor and take a few deep breaths, feeling the connection between your feet and the ground. Imagine roots growing from the soles of your feet, connecting you to the earth. This simple grounding exercise can bring a quick sense of stability and focus.

Integrating Mindfulness into Desk Routines

Sometimes, the best way to practice mindfulness is by incorporating it into your daily tasks. Here are a few ways to weave mindfulness into your work:

Intentional Task Transitions: Before starting a new task, take a deep breath and set a brief intention, like "focus," "clarity," or "patience." This keeps you present and helps create a mental boundary between tasks.

Mindful Drinking or Eating: If you have a cup of coffee or a snack at your desk, take a few moments to savour it. Notice the flavours, textures, and temperature. This small practice can turn a regular break into a calming ritual.

Walking Meditations for Field Employees

For those who work in more dynamic or mobile roles, mindful movement can be a powerful tool for staying centred and maintaining clarity. Walking meditations and mindful movement practices can be done during breaks or between tasks, offering moments of calm and focus.

Walking Meditation

Walking meditation is moving mindfulness that involves paying attention to each step, movement, and breath.

Breath and Step Sync: Try syncing your breath with your steps as you walk. For example, inhale for four steps and exhale for four steps. This can be calming and rhythmic, creating a steady, mindful flow.

Awareness Walk: Notice the physical sensations as you walk—the feeling of your feet on the ground, the swing of your arms, the temperature of the air. Tune into your senses to heighten your awareness of your surroundings, grounding yourself in the moment.

Mindful Observation During Breaks

If you have a few free moments between tasks, use that time for mindful observation.

Nature Connection: Immerse yourself in the surrounding trees, plants, and natural scenery. Observe the colours, textures, and any movements in the wind. This brief connection to nature can boost your mood and refocus your energy.

Object Observation: Choose a small object, like a pen or tool, and inspect it. Notice its weight, colour, texture, and how it feels in your hand. This simple practice can be surprisingly grounding and can help clear your mind.

Mindful Breathing on the Move

Even when moving from place to place, you can practice mindful breathing to keep yourself centred.

Counting Breaths: As you walk, count your breaths up to ten and start over. This simple counting exercise helps you focus on your breath and your movements, grounding you in the present.

Gentle Sigh: If you're feeling tense, take a deep breath and gently sigh as you exhale. Repeat a few times, letting the tension release with each sigh. This can be a quick way to release stress and reset your energy.

Mindfulness doesn't have to take much time—it's all about finding moments to connect with yourself and the present, even on a busy workday. Whether at a desk or on the go, these practices fit into your day, bringing clarity, calm, and focus whenever you need it most. With just a few mindful minutes here and there, you can transform your work environment into a place of balance and awareness.

Chapter 11

ALIGNING WITH NATURE

Nature's rhythms have always been a powerful tool for grounding, guiding, and inspiring people, whether it's the steady cycles of the moon or the changing seasons. In this chapter, we'll explore how to sync your work life with these natural cycles to enhance productivity, creativity, and overall sense of alignment. By using the lunar phases to guide your goal-setting and adjusting your work practices to flow with the seasons, you can create a sense of harmony between your professional life and the natural world around you.

Lunar Phases and Work Goals

The moon has long been a symbol of change and growth, waxing and waning in a predictable cycle. Just as the moon reflects different stages, so can your work life benefit from aligning with the lunar phases. The lunar cycle spans 29.5 days, and its four main phases offer an opportunity to set, track, and reflect on your goals with intention.

New Moon: Setting Intentions for New Beginnings

The New Moon is a time of fresh starts and new possibilities. It's the perfect moment to set intentions for the upcoming month, especially when you're looking to begin a new project, launch a business initiative, or embark on a new direction at work. This phase is all about planting the seeds for future growth, so take time to reflect on what you want to manifest in the coming weeks.

Action Steps:

- Take time on the New Moon to write your intentions. What do you want to achieve? Be clear, concise, and optimistic about your goals.

- Visualize the outcome and set a positive affirmation or mantra that aligns with your work intentions.

- Set clear, actionable steps that you can take over the next month to bring your vision to life.

Waxing Moon: Building Momentum and Taking Action

As the moon grows from the New Moon to the Full Moon, energy builds and strengthens. This phase is to take inspired action and build momentum toward your goals. You've set your intentions; now is the time to move forward with confidence and determination.

Action Steps:

- Focus on making progress by breaking larger tasks into manageable steps. Keep your energy high and be proactive.

- Prioritize tasks that require more energy and effort. This phase is about putting your plans into motion, so tackle those projects you've been putting off.

- Stay organized and track your progress—this is a great time to assess how far you've come.

Full Moon: Celebrating Achievements and Releasing What No Longer Serves You

The Full Moon represents the peak of the lunar cycle, a time to celebrate accomplishments, recognize how far you've come, and take stock of what's working and what's not. It's also a powerful time for releasing anything that no longer aligns with your goals or values—unnecessary work habits, limiting beliefs, or even unproductive relationships.

Action Steps:

- Reflect on what you've achieved so far. Celebrate your wins and acknowledge your progress.

- Reevaluate your goals and the path you've taken. Are there any adjustments or pivots that need to be made? This is a perfect time for reflection.

- Perform a release ritual, either physically (e.g., writing what you want to let go of and burning the paper) or mentally (e.g., meditation on releasing outdated or negative thought patterns).

Waning Moon: Rest, Reflection, and Preparation for the Next Cycle

The Waning Moon is a time for rest, reflection, and preparation for the next cycle. During this phase, energy decreases, so it's important to slow down, reflect on the lessons learned, and prepare for the New Moon. Rather than taking bold action, this is the time to pause and focus on maintaining balance and perspective.

Action Steps:

- Reflect on your progress during the month. Evaluate what worked and what didn't and adjust as needed.

- This is a time for completion and closure. If projects have been lingering, now is the time to wrap them up.

- Use this time to clear your workspace, reset your environment, and restore your energy so you're ready to take action with the New Moon.

By following the natural ebb and flow of the lunar cycle, you can work in harmony with the cosmos, setting a rhythm that supports your goals and allows you to remain grounded and intentional throughout the month.

Seasonal Activities for Work-Life

Besides the lunar cycle, the seasons offer another way to sync your work life with nature's rhythms. Each season brings a unique energy, and aligning your practices with the changing seasons can help you stay balanced, productive, and inspired. Here's how you can adjust your work practices to harmonize with the seasonal shifts.

Spring: Growth, Renewal, and New Projects

Spring is a time of renewal and growth. Nature is waking up from its winter slumber, and so should your creativity and enthusiasm for new projects. This is a time to start something new—launching an initiative, brainstorming fresh ideas, or revitalizing existing goals.

Action Steps:

- Use spring's energy to tackle new projects, take risks, and invest in personal or professional growth.

- Spring-clean your workspace, clearing out old files and clutter to make room for fresh ideas and opportunities.

- Set clear intentions for what you want to bring into your life this season.

Summer: Energy, Action, and Expansion

Summer is a time of high energy, movement, and expansion. It's the season to dive into your work, take action, and focus on productivity. Whether working on a major project or building work relationships, summer offers the perfect energy to push forward and see results.

Action Steps:

- Push forward with ambitious goals and projects. Take advantage of the longer days and higher energy levels to accomplish as much as possible.

- Make time for collaboration, networking, and team-building activities. Summer's warm, outgoing energy is perfect for socializing and expanding your professional connections.

- Stay hydrated and energized with healthy snacks and meals to maintain peak productivity during this active season.

Autumn: Harvest, Reflection, and Adjustments

As the days grow shorter and the air cools, autumn is a time of reflection, harvest, and reaping the rewards of your hard work. This season encourages introspection and adjustment. It's a good time to review your goals, take stock of your progress, and make any necessary tweaks before the year winds down.

Action Steps:

- Reflect on your accomplishments and what you've achieved so far. Celebrate your wins and identify areas for improvement.

- Focus on finishing projects that may have been put on the back burner during the busier months.

- Begin preparing for the quieter, more inward-focused winter season by laying the groundwork for future success.

Winter: Rest, Reflection, and Strategic Planning

Winter is a time of rest, silence, and introspection. While its energy may seem more dormant, this season is crucial for preparing for the year ahead. It's a time to rest, recharge, and plan strategically for the future.

Action Steps:

- Take time off when you can to rest and recharge. The quiet of winter allows for reflection, meditation, and self-care.

- Use the winter months to map out your goals for the coming year, refining strategies and making long-term plans.

- Engage in activities that help nurture your inner world, such as journaling, meditation, or simply spending time in nature.

Aligning with the natural world isn't just about connecting to the earth—it's about understanding and working with the rhythms that shape our lives. By tuning into the cycles of the moon and the changing seasons, you can set goals that feel grounded, inspired, and in harmony with the world around you. This connection to nature helps you create a natural work-life that supports your long-term success.

Chapter 12

INCORPORATING COLOUR MAGIC INTO THE WORK ENVIRONMENT

C olours can shape our moods, productivity, and focus. Incorporating colour magic into your work environment can elevate your space's energy, help set intentions, and create a more harmonious atmosphere. This chapter will guide you through the basics of colour magic and provide practical ways to integrate colours into your workspace with purpose and style.

Understanding Colour Magic

Colour magic is because colours carry specific energies and associations that can influence our feelings and thoughts. Each colour is linked with particular qualities, and by consciously choosing colours, you can bring these energies into your environment to support your work intentions. For example, green promotes balance, while blue enhances focus and calm.

Here's a quick overview of some common colours and their magical associations:

Red: Energy, motivation, courage
Orange: Creativity, enthusiasm, confidence
Yellow: Clarity, joy, positivity
Green: Balance, growth, stability
Blue: Calm, focus, communication

Purple: Intuition, wisdom, transformation
White: Purity, clarity, openness
Black: Protection, grounding, strength

Choosing Colours for Specific Intentions

To incorporate colour magic, consider what qualities would be most beneficial in your work environment. Think about your goals: Do you want to boost focus? Cultivate a calm atmosphere? Stimulate creativity? Once you identify your goals, choose colours that resonate with those intentions.

Here are some examples of colours to match specific work-related intentions:

- Boosting Productivity: Red and yellow can spark energy and focus, keeping you alert and on task.

- Encouraging Creativity: Orange and purple stimulate inspiration and out-of-the-box thinking.

- Promoting Calm: Blue and green bring tranquillity and help reduce stress levels.

- Strengthening Communication: Blue and yellow both support clear, open communication, with blue fostering thoughtfulness and yellow encouraging positivity.

- Instilling Confidence: Red and orange can help you feel more confident and assertive in your interactions.

Practical Ways to Incorporate Colour Magic

Once you've selected the colours that align with your intentions, you can add them to your workspace. Colour magic doesn't require grand gestures—a few intentional touches can make a big difference.

Decor and Accessories

One of the easiest ways to bring colour magic into your workspace is through small decor items and accessories. Consider items like desk organizers, mouse pads, or framed artwork in your chosen colours.

Desk Plants: Add greenery for balance and renewal. Like pothos or jade, plants with dark green leaves bring natural grounding energy.

Crystal Decor: Place crystals in colours that match your intentions. For example, amethyst (purple) can enhance intuition, while citrine (yellow) is excellent for focus and motivation.

Pen Holders and Notebooks: Use coloured accessories to bring your intentions into your daily work tools. A red pen holder for motivation, a blue notebook for clarity and focus, or a yellow mug for positivity can subtly reinforce your goals.

Colourful Clothing and Jewellery

Wear colours that align with your intentions, even if they're subtle. A blue scarf for calm, a yellow tie or blouse for clarity, or a red bracelet for courage can add an intentional energy to your day.

Jewellery with Gemstones: Choose gemstones in your colours of choice, like green aventurine for balance or lapis lazuli for clarity, and wear them as rings, bracelets, or necklaces.

Colourful Socks or Accessories: If you prefer a subtle approach, use accessories like socks or belts. You'll know the colour supports you, even if it's not outwardly visible.

Lighting and Colour Filters

The lighting in your workspace affects the overall energy and ambiance. Try colour-adjustable light bulbs to shift your lighting according to your needs, or use lampshades in specific colours.

Warm Lighting: Soft orange or amber lighting can create a cozy, comforting atmosphere conducive to calming stress.

Cool Lighting for Focus: Blue or white lights stimulate focus and clarity. Use them during times of high concentration.

Colour Filters for Screens: Some people like using screen filters in warm tones to reduce eyestrain, which also brings a subtle energy shift for relaxation.

Creating a Colour Altar or Dedicated Space

If you have room in your workspace, consider setting up a small colour altar or a corner with meaningful items that embody your chosen colours. This dedicated space can serve as a visual anchor for your intentions.

Mini Colour Altar: Arrange a few objects, such as coloured candles, crystals, or small art pieces, that represent your goals. Use this altar as a focal point for a short morning ritual to set intentions, or as a place to centre yourself during breaks.

Seasonal Colour Themes: Change your altar colours with the seasons to stay aligned with natural cycles. For example, greens and pastels in spring, yellows and reds in summer, oranges and browns in fall, and blues and whites in winter.

Colour-Based Visualization Techniques

Visualization exercises can help you connect with the energy of specific colours. Even if your workspace doesn't have physical colour elements, visualizing them can invoke the same intentions.

Visualization for Focus

Take a few deep breaths, and visualize a calm blue light filling your mind and workspace. Picture this colour infusing you with clarity and peace, preparing you for a productive session.

Visualization for Confidence

Imagine a warm red or orange glow radiating from your core, filling you with courage and assertiveness. Visualize this energy expanding outward, helping you feel empowered and ready to tackle challenges.

Respecting Workplace Culture with Subtlety

In some workplaces, using bold colours may not be possible, or you might prefer to keep your colour magic practice private. Here are a few subtle ways to incorporate colour magic:

Invisible Colours: Use colours in your planner, journal, or under your desk. For example, use a yellow highlighter in your notes for clarity or place a purple crystal in a drawer for wisdom.

Small Touches: Select understated items like pens, paperclips, or sticky notes in your chosen colours. These elements can support your intentions while remaining unnoticeable to others.

Digital Backgrounds: Set your computer or phone wallpaper to your focus colour. A calming green or inspiring orange background can serve as a private boost without drawing attention.

Colour Reflection Exercise

At the end of the week, take a moment to reflect on how your colour choices may have influenced your energy and mindset. This practice helps reinforce your understanding of colour magic and allows you to adjust your colours based on your needs.

Reflection Journal: Note any moments when the colours seemed to align with or support your goals. Did the green plant make you feel calmer? Did the yellow mug remind you to stay positive?

Adjustments for the Following Week: Based on your reflections, consider what colours you might add or change to better support your intentions in the coming week.

Colour magic offers an intuitive, approachable way to enhance your workspace. Incorporating colours aligned with your goals and needs brings intention, harmony, and focus to your work environment. Practicing colour magic may make you feel more balanced, energized, and inspired in your daily work life.

Chapter 13

CRYSTALS AND MINERALS IN WORKPLACE MAGIC

C rystals and minerals carry unique energies that can be harnessed for various purposes in the workplace, such as improving focus, protecting against negative influences, and promoting peace. Each crystal or mineral offers its own strengths, allowing you to select stones that align with your intentions. This chapter will explore integrating specific crystals and minerals, including salt, river rock, and sea glass, into your work environment and rituals.

Choosing and Preparing Stones for Work Magic

Selecting crystals and minerals for work starts with setting your intention. Whether you seek protection, clarity, or stress relief, there is a stone to support you. Before bringing any stone into your workspace, consider cleansing it to remove any residual energies and programming it with your intention.

Preparation Techniques:

Cleansing: Run stones under cold water (if the stone is water-safe), pass them through smoke from incense, or leave them in the moonlight overnight.

Programming: Hold the stone in your hand, close your eyes, and visualize your intention, infusing the stone with your goal for its use.

Key Crystals and Minerals for Workplace Magic

Here's a selection of commonly used crystals and minerals to enhance your work life, along with ways to incorporate them into your daily routines.

Clear Quartz

Clear Quartz is the "master healer" and can be used for clarity and focus. It amplifies energy and intentions, making it versatile for a range of workplace purposes.

Use: Keep a small Clear Quartz point or tumbled stone on your desk to promote mental clarity and focus during long work hours. It can also be used to set goals—simply hold the stone as you set your intentions for the day.

Amethyst

Amethyst has a calming energy, making it ideal for stress relief and maintaining mental clarity under pressure. It also promotes intuitive insight, which can be valuable for problem-solving.

Use: Place an Amethyst cluster near your workspace or carry a small tumbled stone in your pocket to stay centred during high-stress situations. An amethyst point facing away from you can help clear negative energy from your workspace.

Salt: A Protective Mineral for Boundaries

Salt has long been associated with cleansing and protection. It's grounding and purifying, which can help create a secure and stable environment in your workspace.

Uses of Salt in the Workplace:

Protective Barrier: Sprinkle a small line of salt along your desk or in a discreet corner to create a barrier that blocks negative energy.

Energy Cleansing: Mix a bit of salt in a bowl of water and keep it near your workspace overnight to absorb negative energy. Discard the water in the morning.

Desk Sachet: Create a small sachet with salt, rosemary, and lavender. Place it in a desk drawer for ongoing energy protection and mental clarity.

River Rock: Stability and Grounding

River rocks, smooth stones shaped by natural currents, carry the grounding, steadying energy of water. They can help you stay centred and calm, especially during times of change or turbulence in the workplace.

Uses of River Rock in the Workplace:

Meditation Aid: Hold a river rock in your hand when you feel scattered or anxious, allowing its grounding energy to bring you back to the present moment.

Stress Relief: Keep a small river rock in your pocket or desk drawer. When feeling overwhelmed, close your hand around it, taking a few deep breaths to reconnect with your sense of stability.

Intentional Focus: Write your weekly intention on a piece of paper and place it beneath the rock on your desk to symbolize steady progress toward your goals.

Sea Glass: Transformation and Flow

Sea glass, often found along beaches, represents transformation and resilience. Its energy is gentle and adaptable, making it a wonderful addition for anyone looking to foster creativity, openness, and a positive mindset in their work.

Uses of Sea Glass in the Workplace:

Creative Inspiration: Place a piece of sea glass on your desk to invite fresh ideas and encourage flexibility in thinking. Its energy reminds you that challenges can lead to beautiful transformations.

Stress Dissipation: When dealing with workplace stress, hold the sea glass and visualize it absorbing the tension. Afterward, rinse it under water to cleanse it.

Harmony: Arrange several pieces of sea glass on your desk to create a mini "zen" display, bringing a calming, beach-like energy to your workspace.

Incorporating Crystals and Minerals into Daily Practices

Here are some simple ways to incorporate crystals and minerals into your daily work life:

Daily Desk Ritual

Each morning, hold your chosen crystal (like Clear Quartz for focus or Amethyst for calm) and take a few deep breaths, setting an intention for the day. This ritual helps align your mind with the crystal's energy and your goals.

Grounding Check-ins

During lunch or a break, take a moment to hold your river rock or salt sachet, focusing on your breath. Visualize any excess stress or anxiety flowing out of you and into the stone, grounding you in the present moment.

Weekly Energy Cleanse

End the workweek by recharging your crystals on a windowsill under sunlight or moonlight. This cleansing ritual helps reset your stone's energy, preparing them for a fresh start the following week.

Choosing the Right Stone for Your Workspace

Each crystal and mineral has unique properties, so choosing the ones that best suit your needs is a matter of preference and goals. By incorporating these stones into your workspace, you bring in natural elements and create an environment that aligns with your intentions and supports your well-being.

Whether you're seeking clarity, protection, grounding, or creativity, the energy of these crystals and minerals can subtly shape your workday, helping you navigate challenges with greater ease and focus. Embrace these tools as quiet, powerful allies in your journey as a Witch at Work, knowing that each stone brings a touch of nature and magic into your professional life.

Chapter 14

LEVERAGING ANIMAL AND MYTHICAL CREATURE MAGIC FOR WORK

Incorporating animal and mythical creature magic into your work life is a powerful way to tap into the unique qualities of these creatures. Whether aspiring for leadership, seeking to develop new skills, or focusing on building teamwork and collaboration, animal symbolism can guide and support your journey. Each creature, real or mythical, embodies specific traits that resonate with different goals and can influence how you approach your work, leadership style, and relationships with colleagues. Here's how you can harness their magic based on your professional aspirations.

Choosing Animal Symbols Based on Career Goals

Each animal carries symbolic meanings that can be aligned with specific professional goals. Here are a few examples:

Aspiring for Leadership: If you're looking to grow as a leader, animals like the eagle, lion, or elephant embody traits of strength, vision, and guidance.

Building Skills and Experiences: Animals like the fox, spider, or octopus are ideal for adaptability, creativity, and learning, helping you embrace a growth mindset.

Fostering Harmony and Teamwork: Animals like dolphins, bees, and wolves emphasize cooperation, communication, and community for those focused on teamwork.

Tip: Choose animals that align with qualities you wish to develop rather than the ones that seem obvious; sometimes, an unexpected animal brings out new, hidden strengths.

Ways to Incorporate Animal Magic in Different Workplaces

Each workplace has its culture and style, which can influence how openly you incorporate animal symbolism. Here are ways to bring animal magic into a variety of work settings:

Corporate Office: Display a small, discreet item representing your chosen animal—such as a feather, a figurine, or a paperweight. Alternatively, keep a symbolic item (e.g., a coin with a specific animal) in your pocket or bag as a talisman.

Remote Work/Home Office: Create an altar or display with animal symbols relevant to your goals. Use wallpaper images of your chosen animal on your computer or phone, or keep a framed picture on your desk as a daily reminder.

Field Work/On-the-Go Jobs: Consider portable items that represent your animal, like a keychain or small charm. In your downtime, visualize your animal and reflect on its qualities. You might also create a small, pocket-sized card with an animal drawing and critical attributes to remind you of your focus.

Tip: In places where objects might be impractical, you can keep the animal symbolism subtle by wearing clothing or accessories representing the energy or colours associated with your chosen animal.

Aspiring Leaders: The Magic of Animal Power and Mythical Leadership

Leadership is not just about managing tasks—it's about inspiring others, making tough decisions, and guiding teams toward shared goals. Animal and mythical creature symbolism can provide the support needed to cultivate these qualities and step into your leadership power.

Animal Symbols for Aspiring Leaders:

Lion—Courage and Authority

Symbolism: Lions are natural leaders, embodying power, courage, and sovereignty. Their presence demands respect and is often seen as a symbol of authority and strength. As a leader, the lion helps you project confidence, make bold decisions, and inspire others to follow your lead.

Leveraging for Work: If you aspire for leadership, channel the lion's energy by exuding self-confidence and authority. Keep a lion figurine or an image on your desk, or visualize a lion standing by your side when preparing for important meetings. The lion helps you tap into your inner power and assert your leadership without hesitation.

Eagle—Vision and Strategy

Symbolism: The eagle represents vision, clarity, and strategic thinking. Known for its ability to soar high and see the big picture, the eagle helps you look beyond immediate challenges and focus on long-term goals.

Leveraging for Work: The eagle's perspective is ideal for those stepping into leadership roles. It reminds you to keep a clear vision and guide your team with wisdom and insight. Before making major decisions, visualize the eagle flying above you, surveying the landscape and helping you gain clarity and foresight.

Mythical Creatures for Aspiring Leaders:

Dragon—Wisdom, Vision, and Leadership

Symbolism: Dragons are symbols of leadership, wisdom, and transformation. As creatures that balance strength with strategic thinking, they are ideal for those stepping into roles of authority or looking to lead in innovative ways.

Leveraging for Work: Invoke the dragon's energy when you need to make bold decisions or inspire transformation within your team. Keep a dragon symbol nearby or meditate on dragon energy to embody strength and visionary leadership. As a leader, channel the dragon's leadership ability with wisdom and passion.

Phoenix—Rebirth and Resilience

Symbolism: The phoenix represents renewal, transformation, and resilience. This mythical bird's ability to rise from its ashes makes it an excellent symbol for those in leadership positions navigating change or facing setbacks.

Leveraging for Work: If you're stepping into a new leadership role or navigating a transition period, the Phoenix can help you embrace change and remain resilient. Visualize the phoenix rising whenever you face challenges as a reminder that setbacks are temporary and can lead to personal and professional growth.

Developing New Skills and Experiences: Animal Allies for Personal Growth

When developing new skills and experiences, you need guidance that helps you embrace learning, overcome obstacles, and build the confidence to try new things. Animal magic can encourage exploration, adaptability, and a growth mindset.

Animal Symbols for Skill Development:

Owl—Wisdom and Intuition

Symbolism: The owl symbolizes wisdom, perception, and intuition. Known for its sharp eyesight and ability to see in the dark, the owl encourages you to seek knowledge and trust your instincts as you explore new areas of expertise.

Leveraging for Work: If you're developing a new skill, whether it's technical or soft skills, call on owl energy for guidance. The owl helps you navigate through challenges with wisdom and insight. Keep an owl figurine on your desk to remind yourself to stay curious, trust your intuition, and be open to learning.

Fox—Adaptability and Cleverness

Symbolism: The fox symbolizes adaptability, cleverness, and resourcefulness. Known for its quick thinking and ability to navigate tricky situations, the fox can help you embrace new challenges with agility and creativity.

Leveraging for Work: As you develop new skills, embrace the fox's energy to stay flexible and quick-witted. Whether learning a new software tool or honing a new management skill, the fox reminds you to approach new situations with cleverness and adaptability. Use the fox's energy to find creative solutions and think on your feet.

Mythical Creatures for Skill Development:

Unicorn—Creativity and Transformation

Symbolism: The unicorn represents creativity, purity, and transformation. It encourages you to embrace your uniqueness and see the world through an innovative lens.

Leveraging for Work: Invoke unicorn energy when you are looking to bring new ideas to your work or develop creative skills. The unicorn helps you embrace transformation, guiding you through personal and professional evolution. Use unicorn imagery or meditations to inspire innovative thinking and explore uncharted territories in your career.

Griffin—Strength and Protection

Symbolism: The griffin, a hybrid of eagle and lion, symbolizes strength, courage, and protection. This mythical creature combines the power of the king of the beasts with the far-reaching perspective of the eagle, making it an excellent ally for overcoming obstacles while developing new skills.

Leveraging for Work: The griffin provides strength and protection when taking on new challenges. If you're trying to master a new skill, invoke the griffin's magic for the strength to push through difficulties. Use its energy to protect your progress and maintain focus as you navigate your learning curve.

Building Teamwork and Collaboration: Animal Allies for Unity

A productive and harmonious team is key to success in any workplace. Animal magic can help you foster collaboration, communication, and mutual respect among your coworkers. Whether you're building a team from the ground up or want to strengthen an existing one, these creatures are powerful allies.

Animal Symbols for Teamwork:

Bee—Teamwork and Collective Effort

Symbolism: Bees are the ultimate symbol of collective effort, cooperation, and teamwork. Each colony member plays a crucial role in achieving the common goal in the bee's world.

Leveraging for Work: Keep a bee symbol nearby to remind yourself of the power of working together. Bees are also great for reminding people that every role contributes to the team's success, no matter how small. As a leader, encourage collaboration by invoking bee magic to build a sense of unity and shared responsibility.

Elephant—Loyalty and Support

Symbolism: Elephants are known for their loyalty, intelligence, and strong sense of family. They work together in herds, offering support to one another during challenging times.

Leveraging for Work: The elephant can be a guiding force in building a supportive, loyal team. Use elephant energy to foster trust and ensure that everyone feels valued. In a leadership role, channel the elephant's wisdom and nurturing qualities to create a workplace where team members look out for one another.

Mythical Creatures for Teamwork:

Pegasus—Freedom and Aspiration

Symbolism: Pegasus, the winged horse, represents freedom, aspiration, and the ability to soar above challenges. This mythical creature is ideal for teams seeking to push the boundaries of their potential and overcome obstacles together.

   Leveraging for Work: Invoke Pegasus's energy when you want to encourage teamwork that thrives on creative freedom and mutual aspiration. Whether you're part of a creative team or a high-performing department, Pegasus encourages everyone to elevate their work and embrace a collaborative spirit that helps everyone rise together.

Faeries—Playfulness and Harmony

Symbolism: Faeries represent balance, harmony, and connection with nature. Known for their joyful and whimsical nature, faeries are great for lightening the atmosphere in a team and fostering a sense of shared joy in collaboration.

   Leveraging for Work: If you're building a team dynamic, faerie magic can bring a sense of joy and cohesion. Invoke faerie energy to encourage playful collaboration, where everyone feels comfortable contributing their ideas and talents. Faeries remind us that work doesn't always have to be serious—it can be fun and still highly productive.

Animal Magic for Every Aspiration

Whether you're looking to step into leadership, develop new skills, or create a harmonious team dynamic, animal and mythical creature, magic provides powerful symbols to guide you in your workplace journey. Each animal and creature has distinct traits that can help you align with your goals, face challenges, and inspire positive change in your environment.

   As you incorporate these symbols and energies into your daily work routine, remember that the magic is not in the creatures themselves but in how you channel their qualities into your actions and mindset.

Whether through meditation, visualization, or physical tokens, animal magic can help you harness the traits of these creatures to create a more empowered, productive, and harmonious work life.

Chapter 15

Embracing the Shadow: Navigating Work Through Self-Discovery

We are asked to bring our best selves to the table in every workplace. Whether we're pushing for promotions, trying to prove ourselves to a team, or balancing the demands of career growth and personal life, we often become experts at presenting a curated image of who we are. But beneath the surface of our conscious, polished personas lies a more profound, often untapped reservoir—our "shadow," a concept introduced by Carl Jung. Shadow work in the workplace is about exploring and integrating these hidden aspects of ourselves: the parts we reject, suppress, or deny.

We all have a shadow. It holds our fears, insecurities, and unresolved emotions—those feelings and traits we often push aside because they don't align with how we aspire to be seen. But by doing shadow work, we can transform these unconscious aspects into strengths. It's through this exploration that we can achieve not only personal growth but also more profound success in our professional lives. The workplace, after all, can be a perfect mirror for understanding our shadow and the places where we need healing, self-awareness, and integration.

Key Aspects of Shadow Work

Self-Reflection

The foundation of shadow work lies in self-reflection. This means diving deep into understanding your motivations, triggers, and behaviours—especially in challenging or heated situations at work. Have you ever noticed how a colleague's offhand comment can throw you off, even when it seems minor? Or how you become defensive when someone critiques your ideas? These reactions often point to unresolved fears or insecurities within yourself. Examining these feelings with curiosity rather than judgment can uncover the parts of your shadow that influence your responses.

Acceptance

The key to shadow work is acceptance. This doesn't mean simply tolerating the parts of ourselves we find uncomfortable or unpleasant. It means recognizing and accepting these traits as a natural part of being human. Whether it's a fear of failure, an inner critic that judges your every move, or impatience that rises in the face of stress, accepting these aspects without shame or guilt helps integrate them into our daily lives in a way that serves us.

Integration

The last step of shadow work is integration. After identifying and accepting our shadows, we can incorporate them into our conscious selves. For example, that fear of failure may highlight an area where you have room to grow or develop more resilience. The key is not to push these traits away, but to acknowledge them and use them as tools for personal development. When you integrate the shadow, you become a more authentic version of yourself with greater clarity and understanding of your motivations and actions.

Applying Shadow Work to the Workplace

Shadow work can be particularly transformative in a work environment. Let's explore how it can be applied across various work contexts, from leadership and career growth to conflict resolution and team dynamics.

Identifying Triggers

Emotional triggers can often be the gateway to understanding our shadows at work. Have you ever felt disproportionately angry or upset in response to a situation or person at work? Perhaps it's a comment from a colleague, an overlooked contribution, or a management decision. These reactions are rarely about the external event itself—they are often a reflection of something within. By identifying what triggers such strong emotions, you can explore what lies beneath the surface. It may point to experiences, a fear of inadequacy, or unresolved issues from earlier in your career. By acknowledging these triggers, you can respond more thoughtfully, preventing unnecessary conflict and promoting better emotional regulation in the workplace.

Recently, as in only a few days ago, I was feeling heavy hearted to the point I had a feeling that tears were about to burst while I was working. I was sad that my twenty year anniversary had just passed with my employer and my manager had not acknowledged it, which is usually done for everyone's anniversaries not just the big ones. I had to acknowledge that I was putting too much weight on my manager's acknowledgement than my own contribution. My sense of self should not come down to a moment in time by an arbitrary person.

Confronting Work-Related Fears

Fears related to failure, judgment, and inadequacy are common in any job. Many professionals hold back from taking risks or stepping into leadership roles because of these deep-seated fears. Shadow work provides the opportunity to confront and work through these fears. Instead of allowing them to paralyze your potential, you can use shadow work to identify their root causes and develop strategies for overcoming them. Perhaps that fear of judgment stems from a childhood experience where your work was criticized. Or maybe the fear of failure arises from an early career misstep that hasn't been fully processed. By confronting these fears head-on, you can transform them into powerful motivators rather than obstacles.

Many of us suffer from imposter syndrome. This is a psychological phenomenon where we doubt our abilities, talents, or accomplishments and fear being exposed as a "fraud." Even when there is evidence of our skills. We often attribute our achievements to luck, timing, or external factors rather than our skills or effort. This can lead to feelings of inadequacy, perfectionism, and anxiety, even in high-performing individuals. It is particularly common in professional or academic settings and can affect anyone, regardless of their level of success or expertise.

Improving Relationships and Teamwork

The shadow also shows up in the ways we relate to others. Traits such as jealousy, impatience, or defensiveness can often arise in team dynamics, especially when conflicts or competition for recognition exist. Shadow work helps you examine these emotions and how they affect your relationships. When you're aware of the negative aspects of your shadow, it's easier to communicate effectively and cultivate more substantial, more empathetic relationships with your colleagues. When you do the internal work to address jealousy, you may find that your interactions become less competitive and more collaborative. This shift can significantly enhance teamwork and foster an environment of mutual respect and understanding.

Enhancing Leadership Skills

For those in leadership positions, shadow work is invaluable. Great leaders can manage their teams and profoundly understand their internal dynamics and biases. Leaders who do the shadow work are more likely to be authentic, self-aware, and empathetic. Shadow work helps them see beyond their biases and unconscious preferences, which can sometimes shape decisions, team dynamics, or even how feedback is given. By confronting their shortcomings, fears, or prejudices, leaders become more attuned to the needs of their teams and can foster a healthier, more inclusive work environment.

Navigating Workplace Conflict

Conflicts in the workplace often involve misunderstandings, miscommunications, and unexamined emotions. You can engage in healthier conflict resolution when you understand your role in a conflict—whether you contributed to escalating tensions or avoided a confrontation. Shadow work allows you to see both sides of an issue and reflect on how unconscious biases or emotions may have influenced your actions. This leads to better problem-solving skills, where solutions are based on genuine understanding and empathy rather than defensiveness or a need to be right.

Setting Authentic Career Goals

One of the biggest benefits of shadow work is its ability to clarify your true motivations. Many people pursue careers based on external expectations, societal pressures, or the desire for validation, but these motivations often leave them feeling unfulfilled. Shadow work invites you to question your underlying values, desires, and passions. When you explore your shadow, you can set goals that align more closely with your true self—goals that lead to personal satisfaction and fulfilment rather than societal approval.

Balancing Work and Personal Life

For some, the shadow manifests as workaholism or a lack of boundaries between work and personal life. Shadow work can help you identify patterns in prioritizing work over self-care or family time. By exploring these patterns, you may uncover a fear of not being enough or a belief that your worth is tied to productivity. Shadow work can help redefine balance, allowing you to set healthier boundaries and prioritize your well-being.

Unlocking Creativity and Innovation

The shadow is also a wellspring of creativity. By acknowledging and integrating your suppressed aspects, you can access new ideas, solutions, and perspectives that you might have ignored or dismissed. Suppressed emotions or ideas—whether they're a creative passion you never pursued or a suppressed desire to challenge the status quo—can spark innovation when brought into the light. Shadow work allows you to explore your repressed parts and find ways to integrate them into your work.

Practical Steps for Applying Shadow Work in the Workplace

Journaling: Keep a journal to reflect on your thoughts, feelings, and workplace experiences. Write about your emotional triggers, fears, and challenging interactions with colleagues.

Mindfulness and Meditation: Use mindfulness techniques to stay present and aware of your thoughts and emotions throughout the workday. This helps you observe your reactions without judgment.

Seek Feedback: Actively request feedback from trusted colleagues or supervisors. Use it as a mirror to examine areas of growth and how you may be unknowingly contributing to workplace dynamics.

Therapy or Coaching: Consider working with a therapist or coach who specializes in shadow work. They can guide you through deeper emotional exploration and help you integrate your discoveries.

Group Discussions: Engage in open, non-judgmental discussions with coworkers about workplace challenges and emotions. This can help create a supportive environment where everyone feels safe to explore their shadows.

Shadow work is not a onetime fix, but a lifelong journey of self-awareness and personal growth. In the workplace, it has the power to transform how we show up in every interaction, decision, and goal we pursue. By exploring our unconscious beliefs, fears, and emotions, we become more authentic, effective, and compassionate in our careers. When we embrace our shadows, we don't just heal ourselves; we heal the environments in which we work, leading to greater fulfilment and success, both personally and professionally.

Chapter 16

SEEING AURAS: INTUITION, EMPATHY, AND CAREER INSIGHT

Throughout history, humans have sought ways to tap into their deeper understanding of the world around them. Whether through tarot cards, astrology, or other spiritual practices, we've long believed in the power to connect with a universal energy. One such concept that has garnered increasing interest in recent years is the ability to see and interpret auras. Auras, often described as a subtle energy field that surrounds all living things, are believed to offer insight into a person's emotional, mental, and spiritual state.

This chapter will explore the art of seeing auras, understanding the significance of different colours, and how this skill can be leveraged in the workplace. We will also discuss the importance of engaging your empathic abilities with caution, avoiding overuse or generalization, and recognizing that intuitive skills like reading people are just one piece of a broader puzzle of interpersonal connection and leadership.

What is an Aura?

An aura is a multi-layered energy field surrounding the body, each layer representing a different aspect of a person's being. Some believe that the colours and qualities of a person's aura reflect their emotional state, thoughts, physical health, and even their spiritual energy. While some people are born with a heightened sensitivity to these energy fields, others can learn to develop this skill through focused practice and awareness.

You may notice subtle colour shifts around a person's body when you see auras. These colours often correspond to different aspects of their personality, current emotional state, or the energy they put into the world.

The Meaning of Different Aura Colours

Although interpreting aura colours can vary slightly depending on spiritual traditions and schools of thought, some common associations can be useful when interpreting them. Here's a breakdown of the most commonly seen colours and their general meanings:

Red: A red aura typically represents strong physical energy, vitality, and passion. It can also indicate someone who is driven, assertive, and action-oriented. In the workplace, a person with a red aura might be seen as a leader or someone with high motivation. However, an overly bright or chaotic red can signal anger or frustration.

Orange: Often associated with creativity, social interaction, and enthusiasm, an orange aura represents a dynamic and confident person. This person may be excellent in collaborative roles, bringing fresh ideas and innovative solutions to the table. If the orange aura is muddied, it could signal unresolved emotions or an overreliance on external validation.

Yellow: A yellow aura is linked to intellect, clarity, and mental acuity. People with yellow auras may excel in roles that require clear thinking, problem-solving, and strategy. They may be seen as analytical and quick-witted, but a pale or an extreme bright yellow might indicate a tendency toward anxiety or overthinking.

Green: Green is often seen as the colour of balance, growth, and healing. Those with green auras are compassionate, empathetic, and nurturing. In a professional setting, individuals with green auras may be excellent in roles that require care, such as healthcare or coaching. However, an overly dark green may indicate jealousy or unresolved emotional issues.

Blue: Blue is the colour of communication, trust, and calm. People with blue auras are often good listeners and strong communicators, making them excellent team players or leaders in roles that require negotiation or mediation. A bright blue can suggest clear expression and emotional stability, while a dull or murky blue might suggest difficulty with self-expression.

Purple: A purple aura is often linked to spirituality, intuition, and deep thinking. Individuals with a purple aura are often seen as visionaries, leaders with a higher perspective. They may thrive in creative or visionary roles in the workplace, such as design or strategy. A dull purple can indicate a need for grounding or an overactive imagination without action.

White: A white aura is often associated with purity, wisdom, and spiritual alignment. It's considered a rare and highly evolved aura. Someone with a white aura will likely be highly intuitive, compassionate, and wise. In a work environment, they may excel in roles that require deep insight, such as counselling or guidance, but they may also be highly sensitive to their surroundings.

Black: While not technically a "colour" of the aura, black in the aura often signifies areas of energetic blockages or emotional turmoil. People with black in their auras may face unresolved inner conflict, pain, or emotional baggage. In the workplace, black in an aura may indicate that the person is experiencing stress, depression, or is holding onto negative emotions that could affect their performance or relationships.

Leveraging Aura Reading in Your Career

Understanding and interpreting auras can be a powerful tool in your professional life, helping you gain deeper insight into the people you work with and the energy of your environment. Here's how you can leverage your ability to see auras in different career contexts:

Enhancing Leadership

If you're in a leadership role, aura reading can help you better understand your team members' emotional states. You can address the issue by recognizing when someone is feeling stressed, anxious, or disengaged (for example, noticing a murky yellow or green aura) before it impacts the team's performance. Leaders who can intuitively sense the energies of those around them are often able to create more harmonious, responsive work environments.

Developing New Skills

Suppose you're looking to develop new skills or take on different responsibilities in your career. In that case, aura reading can help you identify the energies within yourself that may either empower or block your growth. For instance, if your aura lacks vibrant colours like red or yellow, it may indicate that you need to focus on developing more drive or intellectual clarity. Conversely, if you notice your aura is overwhelmed by too much red or orange, it may suggest that you need to balance your approach and slow down to avoid burnout.

Building Teamwork and Collaboration

Reading auras in team settings can help you understand the group's dynamic. If you sense a lot of conflicting energies, such as a mix of yellow (overthinking) and red (aggressive energy), this could point to underlying tensions. Recognizing these dynamics early can facilitate healthier communication and foster a more collaborative, supportive environment. People who can tap into the energies of others often excel in conflict resolution and team building.

Navigating Office Politics

Office politics can be one of the most challenging aspects of any career. Aura reading can provide you with an intuitive understanding of who holds power, who feels insecure, and who may be trying to manipulate situations. If you see an aura filled with heavy black or dark green tones around a colleague, it might be a sign of jealousy, resentment, or personal conflict that could be affecting their behaviour. Understanding these dynamics allows you to protect yourself emotionally and respond strategically.

How to Develop Aura Reading

Learning to read auras is less about having a natural gift and more about culti-vating awareness and sensitivity to the energy surrounding individuals. Whether you are naturally attuned to subtle energies or entirely new to the concept, the following steps can help you develop the ability to perceive and interpret auras.

Grounding and Centreing

Before attempting to read auras, ensure you are calm and grounded. Practices like meditation, deep breathing, or visualizing roots connecting you to the Earth can help anchor your energy, making it easier to sense others' fields.

Practice Peripheral Vision

Auras are often visible through peripheral vision rather than direct focus. Begin by softly gazing at a person or object with a plain background. Let your eyes relax and notice any subtle colours, light, or vibrations around you.

Start with Your Own Aura

Hold your hand against a neutral background and focus on the space beyond your fingers. With practice, you may notice a faint outline or shimmer. Observing your own aura helps build confidence before reading others.

Use an Aura-Friendly Environment

Lighting can significantly impact aura perception. Dimly lit spaces or natural light tend to work best. Avoid overly bright or colourful environments that can distract from subtle energy fields.

Pay Attention to Sensations

Auras can also be "felt" rather than seen. As you focus on someone's energy, notice any changes in temperature, tingling, or emotional shifts you experience. These physical or emotional cues often provide valuable insight into their energy field.

Work with Tools

Crystal pendulums, aura photography, or energy visualization techniques can be training wheels for developing this skill. Over time, these tools become less necessary as your intuitive abilities strengthen.

Practice with Willing Partners

Ask friends or family members if you can practice reading their auras. Share what you perceive and compare notes to gain deeper understanding and validation.

What If You Cannot See Auras?

Not everyone perceives auras visually, and that's perfectly okay! Aura reading is about connecting with energy, and there are multiple ways to sense and interpret it:

Feeling Auras

Energy fields can be felt physically or emotionally. You might notice warmth, coolness, tingling, or even emotional waves as you tune into someone's aura. Trust these sensations—they're just as valid as visual perceptions.

Listening for Auras

Some people "hear" auras as vibrations, tones, or even words that come to mind intuitively. This auditory form of aura reading is less common but equally powerful for those who experience it.

Using Intuition

If you can't see or feel auras, use your intuitive senses. Focus on a person and ask yourself:

- What emotions or impressions do I pick up from their energy?

- Do I sense any specific colours, even if I don't see them?

- How do I feel when I'm around them?

Often, your intuition can provide insights beyond what you might see or feel physically. Trust your intuition if not biased. Biases can influence our intuition if in doubt be open to learning more about a situation or person before making any judgements.

Energy Mapping

If you cannot read an aura directly, create an "energy map" by observing someone's behaviour, speech, and body language. These outward expressions are often reflections of their inner energy and can guide your understanding of their aura.

Be Patient and Practice

Aura reading, like any skill, takes time to develop. If it doesn't come naturally, don't get discouraged. The more you practice, the more attuned you'll become to the subtle energy fields surrounding you.

Remember, seeing auras is not the only way to connect with energy. Trust your unique abilities and embrace the path that feels most natural to you.

Empathy and Caution: Avoiding Overuse or Generalization

While aura reading can be an incredibly valuable tool, it's important to approach this skill with care. First and foremost, it's essential to avoid overuse or generalizing what you perceive. Auras are fluid and can change throughout the day based on emotions, health, and even external influences. A person who appears to have a murky green aura one moment may shift to a brighter, more vibrant colour after a conversation or change in mood.

Empathy plays a critical role in reading auras, but it's crucial not to overstep boundaries or make assumptions about people based solely on their energy. What you perceive is not necessarily the entire truth of that individual. People are complex, and while auras can provide insight into their current emotional state, they do not completely define who they are. Moreover, it's important not to project your own feelings or expectations onto others when interpreting their aura.

Lastly, always be cautious not to overwhelm yourself with the emotional energy of others. If you find yourself becoming drained or overly affected by the surrounding auras, it may be a sign to take a step back, practice grounding exercises, and ensure that you're not absorbing more than you can handle. Maintaining healthy boundaries is crucial when using intuitive abilities in the workplace.

Seeing and interpreting auras is a unique gift that, when used responsibly, can provide significant insight into the people around you and the dynamics at play in your professional life. By learning to read the subtle energy fields of others, you can improve your leadership abilities, foster teamwork, navigate conflicts, and make informed decisions based on a deeper understanding of human emotions.

However, as with any intuitive skill, it's essential to approach aura reading with caution and discernment. Avoid generalizing based on what you perceive and always be mindful of the energy you bring into the room. The power to read auras can enhance your empathy and intuition, but like all tools, it must be used with care and wisdom for maximum effectiveness.

Chapter 17

DAILY RITUALS FOR SUCCESS

S tarting and ending the workday with intentional rituals can be a powerful way to align your energy, set goals, and release stress. Morning and evening rituals can help to ground your day, providing structure, motivation, and clarity. This chapter will guide you through creating personal rituals that are quick, effective, and easy to integrate into your daily routine.

Wake-up Rituals No Matter Your Schedule:

Perhaps you are the sort of person who wakes up alert and ready to start the day, or you may be on the other side of the scale, like me, where you want to hit the snooze button, snuggle down deeply in the mattress, and pretend it is a holiday. But most of us don't get paid to sleep and can't work from bed.

The start of your day, whenever that may be, sets the tone for what's coming. You can begin with a clear and positive mindset by dedicating a few moments to grounding yourself and setting intentions. These rituals help you transition from rest to action, sparking motivation and focus. These techniques can be leveraged on work and non-work days.

The Rituals to Avoid—Our Technology

I'm guilty. I admit I get into a pattern of looking at my cell phone first thing in the morning. Like most of us, our cell phone is often our alarm clock, forcing us to acknowledge its presence when we hear the intrusive sound.

For a time, I checked my work emails before I even sat-up in bed. Often resulting in frustration brewing in the days to come. If I opened some form of social media, I could lose precious minutes going down rabbit holes of real and fake happenings. Then, one morning, I realized how off-putting my day was because of the initial onslaught my phone brought me each morning. I still use it as my alarm clock, but I make a point not to unlock the screen until I am in a better place to tackle the day.

How to Use the Snooze Button

Perhaps it's just me, but I feel a little powerful when I hit snooze on my alarm. It is like telling the world it can't boss me around. However, instead of endless cycles of hitting snooze and just drifting back to sleep to be interrupted again, I take a different approach.

I set the alarm time allowance for one snooze. When the alarm goes off and I smack that button, but I don't fall back asleep. Instead, I slowly start waking up my mind and body.

It starts with turning on a light. I have a remote button for the ceiling light, but an end table light would also work. I welcome the light into my morning, but depending on your schedule, it could be your afternoon, evening, or night. I do some organic stretching movements, whatever feels comfortable. My stretches are slow, and I imagine waking up the tissues in my muscles. From personal experience, an aggressive toe stretch could result in a calf cramp.

Along with some stretches, I will do a few breathing exercises. I prefer the 4-4-8+ breathing in for four, holding for four, and breathing out for eight or more beats, really slow on the out-breath.

Other methods of waking the body include visualization exercises and muscle contractions and releases. The goal is to be awake enough to get out of bed before or when the snooze alarm rings again.

Setting Daily Intentions and Affirmations

An intention is a guiding principle or purpose you want to carry through your day. It can be a single word—like calm, focus, confidence—or a specific goal, such as "Today, I will approach challenges with patience."

Centre Yourself: Find a comfortable place to sit or stand. Take three deep breaths, inhaling through the nose and exhaling through the mouth. Visualize any lingering sleepiness or worries leaving your body.

Choose Your Intention: Close your eyes and consider what you want to feel or accomplish today. Acknowledge any anxieties or stresses that might lie ahead, and find an intention that can support you through them. Examples might be:

- "Today, I am capable and focused."

- "I approach every interaction with compassion and understanding."

- "I am open to new possibilities."

Repeat and Reinforce: Once you've selected an intention, repeat it to yourself silently or aloud. Imagine this intention spreading through your body, energizing you for the day.

Affirmations for Empowerment: Write down or say three positive affirmations that align with your goals. Try one of these, or create your own:

- "I am ready to face the day with resilience and clarity."

- "I trust my abilities to overcome challenges."

- "Today, I bring my best self to my work."

Keep these affirmations somewhere visible (on a sticky note, on your phone, or in your planner) for a quick mental boost throughout the day.

Energizing Morning Beverages-Add a Little Zing

A ritualistic wake-up drink can boost your body and mind and set the tone for a productive day. Here are two energizing beverage recipes with ingredients promoting focus and alertness.

Golden Turmeric Latte: A warming, vibrant drink with antioxidants and anti-inflammatory properties.

Ingredients:

- 1 cup of almond milk (or any milk of your choice): wisdom, growth, and abundance.

- 1/2 tsp turmeric powder: healing, protection, and purification.

- 1/4 tsp cinnamon: passion, prosperity, protection, and spirituality.

- 1/4 tsp ginger powder: strength, courage, and success.

- 1 tsp honey or maple syrup (optional): honey - sweetness and attraction or maple syrup - sustainability, balance, and abundance.

- A pinch of black pepper: banishing negativity, protection, and purification.

Instructions:

1. Heat the milk in a small saucepan over medium heat.

2. Add the turmeric, cinnamon, ginger, and black pepper. Whisk well.

3. Pour into a mug, sweeten if desired, and enjoy your morning boost!

Matcha Mint Smoothie: Matcha, known for its gentle caffeine content and antioxidants, combines with mint to create a refreshing morning drink.

Ingredients:

- 1 tsp matcha powder: vitality, focus, and renewal.

- 1/2 cup almond milk: wisdom, growth, and abundance.

- 1/2 banana: fertility, prosperity, and happiness.

- 1/4 cup fresh spinach: strength, healing, and grounding.

- A few fresh mint leaves: cleansing, protection, and prosperity.

- Ice cubes.

Instructions:

    1. Blend all ingredients until smooth.

    2. Pour into a glass and enjoy as you reflect on your intentions.

Any Time-of-Day Ritual for Cleansing and Refresh

I was a teenage when a nurse at our high school first introduced me to this ritual. She was training some of us to be peer counsellors and said that sometimes what we hear or experience might be too much and that we should not bring it home. As a professional, she created a ritual to wash her hands after something distressing or at the end of her shift so she would not bring home the weight of the day.

Feel the water wash over your hands and across your fingers as you wash them. Envision it, washing away the images, feelings, and discomfort. See the water circle and flow down the drain, taking the weight of a situation or day. If you are free to do so, express your emotions; cry or sob if the day felt blue, yell if the day forced you to bite your tongue and hide a portion of yourself. Give yourself permission to feel and release.

Washing your hands doesn't solve a problem but helps put it in perspective and lower its priority. It also gives you a few minutes to re-centre and collect your thoughts. For example, if your job was in telephone customer service and you just had a really bad call. Taking two to three minutes to wash your hands could reset you enough to tackle the next call. If you were a caregiver and experienced someone in pain that would could not alleviate you may benefit from a moment or two to release the internal guilt you may feel.

End-of-Day Rituals for Reflection and Release

After a long day, end-of-day rituals are an opportunity to reflect on accomplishments, release stress, and reset for tomorrow. These calming practices will help you to let go of any tension and foster a restful mindset.

Reflection Practices: Journaling and Gratitude

Reflecting on your day allows you to process unresolved feelings, recognize progress, and set future intentions.

Journaling Prompts for Reflection:

- What went well today? Write down one or two things that made your day better, no matter how small.

- What challenged me? Reflecting on challenges can give you clarity and help prepare you to handle similar situations in the future.

- What am I grateful for? Identifying a few things you're thankful for can improve your mood and reduce stress.

Gratitude Practice:

Write down three things you are grateful for in a journal or notebook, focusing on what truly brought you joy or comfort that day. This could be something as simple as a pleasant conversation, a delicious meal, or a quiet moment to yourself.

End your journaling with an affirmation for the next day, such as "I am ready to wake up refreshed and ready to tackle new opportunities."

Calming Evening Recipes for Relaxation

Enjoying a soothing drink or snack in the evening can signal your body that it's time to wind down. Here are two relaxing recipes perfect for your end-of-day ritual.

Calm and Clarity Chamomile Tea: Chamomile is known for its calming effects, making it ideal for winding down.

Ingredients:

- 1 tsp dried chamomile flowers or a tea bag: calm, peace, and protection. As well as ward off negative energy.

- ¼ cup of orange juice: vitality, joy, and creativity.

- 1 cup boiled/hot water: purification, healing, and emotional flow.

- Honey, to taste (optional): sweetness and attraction.

Instructions:
1. Steep the tea bag or flowers in a tea diffuser in hot water for 5–7 minutes, then remove the bag or infuser.

2. Add the orange juice.

3. Sweeten with honey if desired.

4. Sip slowly, letting the warmth relax you.

Calming Oat and Nut Bars: These bars are full of magnesium and B vitamins, which help relax the nervous system and prepare you for a good night's sleep.
Ingredients:
- 1 cup oats: nourishment, abundance, and grounding

- 1/2 cup almond butter: binding, wisdom, growth, and abundance

- 1/4 cup honey or maple syrup: honey - sweetness and attraction or maple syrup - sustainability, balance, and abundance

- 1/4 cup chopped almonds: wisdom, growth, and abundance

- 1/4 cup dried cherries or cranberries: cherries - love, passion, and fertility or cranberries - protection, healing, and renewal

Instructions:
1. Mix all ingredients in a large bowl until combined.

2. Press the mixture into a parchment-lined baking dish.

3. Refrigerate for an hour, then cut into bars.

4. Store in the fridge and enjoy as a relaxing evening snack.

These daily rituals help you cultivate a sense of balance and intention throughout your day. Morning rituals prepare you for a fresh start, while evening practices create a peaceful transition to rest. Experiment with these ideas, and remember to adjust them to fit your lifestyle and unique energy.

Chapter 18

WEEKLY RITUALS FOR BALANCE

Setting up weekly rituals brings a sense of rhythm to the workweek, helping you stay aligned with your goals while maintaining a sense of personal balance. These beginning and end-of-week practices foster clarity, motivation, and calm, making it easier to move through the week with purpose and to leave behind stress as you enter the weekend.

Beginning of Week Intention Setting

Starting the week with intention sets a proactive, focused tone that can carry you through even the busiest days. Taking a few moments on Sunday evening or Monday morning to set goals and visualize your week helps you mentally prepare and prioritize your efforts.

Rituals for Goal Setting and Vision Boarding on Sunday or Monday

Intention setting can be as simple as writing a few goals for the week or as elaborate as creating a mini vision board. This process is about identifying what you want to achieve professionally and personally and committing to a mindset that supports those goals.

Goal-Setting Rituals:

Weekly Goals List: Write three to five goals for the week. These could be related to specific work tasks, personal growth, or well-being practices. Keep this list visible as a reminder of your priorities.

Mini Vision Board: Cut out images or phrases from magazines or print out words and pictures that capture your aspirations for the week. This creative ritual helps bring your intentions to life in a visual format.

Morning Affirmation: To set a positive tone, choose an affirmation such as "I am capable and resilient" or "I move through the week with purpose and calm. "

Journaling and Visualization Practices

Journaling and visualization are powerful tools to build focus and excitement for the week ahead. By putting thoughts to paper and visualizing outcomes, you create a mental map for success.

Ideas for Journaling and Visualization:

Weekly Prompt: Reflect on what you want to achieve and why it matters. Write about any challenges you anticipate and how you plan to overcome them.

Future-Self Visualization: Imagine yourself having accomplished your goals at the end of the week. Picture the satisfaction and pride you feel. This exercise reinforces your commitment and boosts your confidence.

Intention Journal: Dedicate a small journal to weekly intentions. Record your goals, affirmations, or vision for each week to build a ritual of focused planning.

End-of-Week Reflection and Release

As the weekends, it's helpful to take time for reflection and self-care. Celebrating your achievements and releasing stress allows you to end the week positively, leaving you refreshed and ready for the weekend.

Friday Rituals to Celebrate Accomplishments and Release Stress

Taking stock of your progress and recognizing even small wins helps you wrap up the week with closure and achievement. Releasing stress is equally important, allowing you to step away from work and recharge.

Ideas for End-of-Week Reflection:

Achievement List: Jot down three accomplishments, large or small. Reflect on your steps to reach these wins, and feel proud of your effort.

Gratitude Practice: Write things you're grateful for during the week. Gratitude can improve mood and put challenges into perspective.

Symbolic Release: Write any worries or unresolved issues on a slip of paper, then crumple or tear it up. This simple ritual signals to your mind that you're letting go.

Self-Care Activities to Recharge Over the Weekend

The weekend offers a valuable opportunity to rest and replenish. Incorporating intentional self-care activities helps you recover from the week's demands, fostering a balanced, grounded state as you prepare to start anew.

Weekend Recharge Ideas:

Digital Detox: Spend time away from screens. Engage in activities that help you reconnect with yourself, such as reading, spending time outdoors, or pursuing a hobby.

Pampering Ritual: Dedicate time to self-care practices like a warm bath, skincare routine, or gentle yoga to release tension and nourish your body.

Nature Walk or Meditative Stroll: Take a walk in a park or natural setting, paying attention to the sights and sounds around you. This helps ground your energy and bring a sense of calm.

Weekly rituals not only structure goals and accomplishments but also help you maintain a healthy work-life balance. Setting intentions at the beginning of the week and reflecting at the end creates a positive cycle of focus, progress, and renewal, supporting your personal and professional growth.

Chapter 19

FOOD AS FUEL

Our food choices shape our energy, focus, and overall well-being—especially during the workday when we need mental clarity and stamina. By incorporating mindful eating and a dash of kitchen magic, you can transform your meals into tools for productivity and intention-setting. This chapter will guide you through energizing recipes, ingredient correspondences, and practices that can turn everyday meals into sources of motivation and inspiration.

Recipes for Focus and Clarity

Certain foods are known for their brain-boosting qualities, helping focus, memory, and mental clarity. These recipes combine ingredients that are both nutritionally supportive and aligned with productivity intentions.

Brain-Boosting Snacks and Meal Ideas

Here are some simple, energy-boosting options that can keep you sharp and focused throughout the day:

Nutty Berry Parfait

Ingredients: Greek yogurt, a handful of walnuts, mixed berries, a sprinkle of chia seeds, and a drizzle of honey.

Benefits: Walnuts are packed with omega-3s for brain health, berries contain antioxidants that improve memory, and chia seeds provide a steady energy release.

Magical Correspondences: Honey represents clarity and focus, walnuts for wisdom, and berries for protection and grounding. Enjoy this parfait as a light, nourishing breakfast or a mid-morning snack to set a focused, positive tone.

Green Goodness Smoothie

Ingredients: Spinach, banana, almond milk, a spoonful of almond butter, and a dash of cinnamon.

Benefits: Spinach provides iron and antioxidants, while bananas and almond butter offer steady energy. The addition of cinnamon can improve focus and alertness.

Magical Correspondences: Bananas symbolize happiness, spinach represents vitality, and cinnamon offers protection and clarity. Sip this smoothie as a quick breakfast or an afternoon pick-me-up.

Savoury Trail Mix

Ingredients: Almonds, pumpkin seeds, sunflower seeds, dark chocolate chips, and dried rosemary or sage.

Benefits: Almonds and seeds provide healthy fats, proteins, and essential nutrients, while a bit of dark chocolate gives a subtle energy boost.

Magical Correspondences: Rosemary brings mental clarity, almonds for prosperity and wisdom, and pumpkin seeds for confidence and grounding. This mix is perfect for a quick, satisfying snack at your desk.

Mindful Eating Practices

Bringing mindfulness into your eating habits helps you enjoy your food more and aligns your energy with your work intentions. Mindful eating encourages you to pause, reflect, and treat food as part of your self-care routine, which can make a surprising difference in your day-to-day focus and well-being.

Encouraging Mindfulness in Food Choices at Work

Pause and Set an Intention: Before you dive into your meal or snack, take a moment to breathe and set an intention. For example, if you're having a salad, you might focus on receiving nourishment and energy, envisioning the greens and veggies fuelling you for the tasks ahead.

Eat Without Distractions: Avoid eating at your computer or while scrolling on your phone. Take a few minutes to focus solely on your food, noticing the flavours and textures. This practice makes eating more enjoyable and promotes better digestion and focus.

Connecting Nutrition with Self-Care and Daily Intentions

Daily Intentions Through Food: You can approach meals with specific intentions tied to your work goals. For example, if you're starting a creative project, choose foods associated with inspiration and creativity, like oranges (for joy) or almonds (for focus).

Gratitude Rituals: Before meals, spend a few seconds expressing gratitude for the food, the effort it took to prepare it, and how it will nourish your body. You might also silently thank each ingredient for its unique benefits and energy.

Magical Correspondences of Ingredients for Enhancing Productivity

Many foods have traditional correspondences in magical practices, with certain ingredients believed to support focus, clarity, and even creativity. Here's a list of commonly available ingredients and their magical qualities, which you can incorporate into your meals with purpose.

Rosemary: Known for mental clarity and focus, rosemary can be used in small amounts in teas or as a seasoning for roasted vegetables or soups.

Lemon: A symbol of purification and mental clarity, lemon can be added to water or used as a zesty snack.

Basil: This herb is associated with prosperity and focus. Adding fresh basil to salads, sandwiches, or even a simple pasta dish can boost focus and help create a positive, abundant mindset.

Almonds: A nut with strong ties to wisdom and insight, almonds can be eaten as a snack or added to smoothies and parfaits.

Ginger: Known for its energizing and grounding qualities, ginger can add a warm flavour to meals, from stir-fries to teas, giving you a boost of motivation.

Cinnamon: Often used for clarity and protection, cinnamon's warm, spicy flavour is a great addition to morning oats or sprinkled over fruit for an extra focus boost.

Using these ingredients with intention can help you infuse daily meals with purpose, aligning your food with your goals and state of mind.

You can support productivity, creativity, and focus by thoughtfully incorporating foods that fuel both body and mind. Simple choices like adding cinnamon to your morning oats or snacking on a rosemary-infused trail mix can create subtle but powerful shifts in how you approach the day's challenges. By making mindful eating a regular part of your routine, you're taking an extra step in aligning with your best, most energized self.

Chapter 20

BUILDING COMMUNITY

C reating a sense of community at work goes beyond simply collaborating on projects. When we can support each other's growth, celebrate each other's wins, and navigate challenges together, the workplace becomes a space of shared purpose and connection. This chapter explores how to foster a sense of belonging and teamwork by incorporating collaborative rituals and forming support circles. These practices can help build an environment where everyone feels motivated, valued, and empowered to succeed.

Collaborative Rituals

Bringing ritual into the workplace may sound unconventional, but it can be as simple as setting shared goals, holding a group meditation, or celebrating milestones together. Collaborative rituals foster a sense of unity, making it easier for teams to work in harmony and support each other's growth. Here are some ways to build connection and intention through ritual.

Setting Collective Intentions

Starting the week or month with a shared intention can set a powerful tone for the team. By aligning on a common goal or value, everyone feels part of something bigger than their individual tasks. It could be something as straightforward as focusing on "excellence in service" or "supporting each other's success," giving the team a focal point to rally around.

Action Steps:

- Gather the team for a short meeting at the beginning of each week or month to discuss a common intention.

- Ask everyone to contribute one word or phrase that captures their personal goals for the period.

- Combine these intentions into a shared statement that serves as a reminder of the team's collective vision.

Goal-Setting Sessions

When done as a group, goal-setting becomes more than just a list of objectives—it transforms into a ritual of support and accountability. This can be particularly effective for long-term projects, as it allows everyone to break down their tasks, share their progress, and feel encouraged by others' commitment.

Action Steps:

- Schedule regular goal-setting sessions, where each person shares their primary goals and the steps they'll take to achieve them.

- Encourage a culture of positive reinforcement by inviting team members to share constructive feedback and support.

- Close the session with a moment of reflection, where everyone envisions the successful completion of their goals.

Celebrating Wins and Milestones

Celebrating accomplishments, big or small, brings the team together and acknowledges everyone's hard work. Ritualizing these celebrations makes them even more meaningful, transforming them from casual congratulations into moments of recognition and gratitude.

Action Steps:

- At the end of a project or upon reaching a key milestone, reflect on everyone's contributions.

- Create a small ritual for recognition, like a team toast or giving out a small symbolic token (a "success stone" that moves from person to person, for example).

- Use these moments to affirm the team's strengths and express gratitude, boosting morale and creating a lasting bond.

Support Circles in the Workplace

A support circle offers encouragement, accountability, and mutual assistance. It can become a powerful resource for personal and professional development in a professional setting. By building a support circle, you create a network that helps everyone grow, adapt, and navigate challenges together.

Forming Accountability Groups

Accountability groups work best when members are aligned with their goals and are comfortable providing and receiving constructive feedback. An accountability group might focus on skill development, project completion, or personal growth in a work context. Regular check-ins ensure each member stays on track and feels supported in achieving their objectives.

Action Steps:

- Start by inviting colleagues interested in forming an accountability group to a brainstorming session. Discuss the goals and support each person would find helpful.

- Set up regular meeting times, whether weekly, biweekly, or monthly, where everyone shares their progress and any challenges they're facing.

- Encourage open, nonjudgmental discussion and ensure each person gets equal time to share. Close each session with encouragement or action items for the next meeting.

Creating Professional and Personal Support Networks

Support circles can focus on both personal and professional topics, creating a balanced space for team members to share work-related goals and issues that affect their overall well-being. These networks are valuable for team members who might feel isolated, especially in larger workplaces or remote settings.

Action Steps:

- Form small groups where colleagues with similar interests or roles can discuss their experiences, goals, and strategies for success.

- Designate each meeting with a theme or focus, such as "stress management," "career development," or "work-life balance," to provide structure and purpose.

- Encourage group members to offer solutions, share resources, and actively listen, creating a supportive environment that feels safe and inclusive.

Creating Rituals for Team Support

Building a community isn't just about working together—it's about supporting each other through life's highs and lows. Rituals that reinforce team support, whether celebrating birthdays or acknowledging tough times, add a layer of humanity to the workplace and foster genuine care among colleagues.

Action Steps:

- Celebrate special occasions and personal milestones, such as birthdays or work anniversaries, with small, personalized gestures (e.g., a team card, a favourite treat, or a thoughtful message).

- Create a "support board" or digital space where team members can anonymously share challenges or requests for encouragement.

- Establish a team "support hour" once a month, during which anyone can bring up personal or work-related concerns and receive advice and support from the group.

Creating a workplace community isn't just about collaboration—it's about forming meaningful connections and fostering an environment of mutual respect, trust, and support. Through rituals, support circles, and shared intentions, you can build a team that thrives together, encourages one another, and grows stronger daily. These practices turn the workplace into more than a location—a sanctuary of collaboration, growth, and shared purpose.

Chapter 21

RELIANCE VS. RESILIENCE IN WORKPLACE WITCHCRAFT

In the fast-paced, ever-evolving workplace environment, the balance between reliance and resilience is essential for those who integrate witchcraft and magical practices into their careers. The ability to rely on external magical tools and rituals can be empowering. Still, the resilience built through personal growth, adaptability, and responsibility will sustain a successful career in the long run. Understanding how to balance these two concepts can help work witches tap into their full potential while ensuring they remain grounded, proactive, and fully engaged with their professional journey.

Reliance: The Allure of External Magic

Reliance in workplace witchcraft refers to the dependence on external sources—magical tools, spells, rituals, or objects—to manifest the desired outcomes. For work witches, this often involves using spells for protection, crystals for energy balancing, or herbs for clarity and focus. These tools can provide immediate comfort and guidance, offering quick fixes to problems and frustrations that arise in a professional setting. However, it is crucial to understand the implications of relying too heavily on these external sources.

The Drawbacks of Reliance

Short-Term Solutions: Magical tools can indeed provide relief and solutions in the short term. A well-cast spell for job promotion or a carefully chosen crystal for focus may bring immediate benefits. However, this approach focuses on quick results rather than sustainable, long-term growth. Over time, relying too much on magic can prevent the work witch from addressing the underlying issues, whether skill development, interpersonal conflicts, or systemic challenges at work.

Avoiding Responsibility: One of the biggest risks of over-relying on magic is the tendency to abdicate responsibility for personal actions. When the expectation is that magic alone can shape success, it's easy to forget that professional growth requires effort, self-reflection, and accountability. If a work-witch views magic as a substitute for hard work or the development of practical skills, they will encounter stagnation in their career.

Disconnection from Practicality: While magic is undeniably powerful, it doesn't replace the real-world efforts required to thrive professionally. Teamwork, communication, and technical skills are foundational to success in any career. By focusing too much on magical tools and rituals, work-witches may find themselves disconnected from the practical aspects of their work. The balance between the magical and the practical is essential to avoid this disconnection.

Resilience: The Power of Personal Agency

Resilience refers to the ability to adapt, recover, and thrive in the face of challenges. For a work-witch, resilience involves recognizing that magic can support their efforts, but that genuine success lies in their agency, decision-making, and personal growth. Resilience in workplace witchcraft emphasizes a balanced, holistic approach to using magic while actively engaging with the demands of the professional world.

The Benefits of Resilience

Empowerment and Agency: A resilient work-witch understands that while magical practices can provide clarity, guidance, and energy, it is their own decisions, actions, and contributions that ultimately shape their career. This mindset encourages a sense of empowerment and ownership. By focusing on resilience, a work-witch fosters the belief that their success or failure isn't dictated solely by the spells they cast or the crystals they use—it is about their work ethic, adaptability, and willingness to face challenges head-on.

A Holistic Approach: Resilience invites a holistic approach to professional success. It integrates magical practices as one of many tools to support growth while remaining open to learning new skills, networking, and honing communication strategies. When magic is part of a broader personal development strategy, it becomes a valuable ally rather than a crutch.

Adaptability: Resilient work witches understand the dynamic nature of the workplace. External circumstances change—new challenges arise, job demands evolve, and team dynamics shift. A resilient witch embraces flexibility and adapts their magical practices to meet these changes. Instead of relying on the same ritual or spell to solve every problem, a resilient witch develops the skill of shifting their magical tools as needed, blending them with practical solutions.

Striking the Balance: How to Integrate Reliance and Resilience

To successfully integrate magic into the workplace without falling into the trap of reliance or the passivity of external tools, work-witches must strive for a balance that incorporates both reliance and resilience. Below are some strategies for achieving this balance:

Empowerment Through Practice: Magic can be an empowering force in the workplace, boosting confidence and clarity. Use spells or rituals to clear away self-doubt and enhance focus, but always remain proactive in taking steps toward your goals. For example, you might use a spell for protection before a big meeting. Still, it's equally important to prepare thoroughly for the meeting, engage thoughtfully with your colleagues, and follow up with actionable steps.

Integrative Rituals: Combine magical elements with practical, actionable strategies. For example, during a new moon ritual, set intentions for professional growth, but complement that with concrete steps such as taking on a new project, seeking a mentor, or upskilling. This combination ensures that you are engaging both your magical and practical resources.

Mindful Reflection: Regular reflection is key to ensuring that magical practices serve your professional development in a balanced way. Take time each week to assess your approach—are you relying too much on spells for outcomes you could achieve through skill-building? Are you engaging with your magical tools as a means of empowerment or avoiding the hard work required to make progress? This self-awareness will guide you toward more intentional, resilient practices.

Community and Support: As a work-witch, connecting with others who understand the balance between magic and professional growth can be invaluable. Join a community of like-minded individuals who can share experiences, offer advice, and encourage one another to stay grounded and resilient in the workplace. Engaging in these communities reinforces the importance of personal agency while celebrating the magical tools at your disposal.

Continuous Learning: Magic is an ever-evolving practice, and so is your career. Keep learning and growing in both areas. While your magical practices will continue to evolve, so should your professional skills. Resilience recognizes that challenges are growth opportunities, whether magical or professional. By continuously learning from your successes and setbacks, you strengthen your capacity for resilience.

A Balanced Path Forward

The interplay between reliance and resilience is one of the most significant aspects of workplace witchcraft. When used as a supportive tool rather than a crutch, magic can be a powerful ally in navigating professional challenges. However, genuine success lies in the ability to integrate magical practices with resilience, ensuring that you always take personal responsibility for your actions, adapt to new circumstances, and grow both spiritually and professionally.

Work-witches who balance reliance and resilience will be equipped to thrive in the workplace. They will use magic as a guiding force while remaining firmly grounded in their own agency and efforts. This approach fosters a career filled with empowerment, creativity, and sustainable success—in which magic is an invaluable tool but is never the sole determinant of success.

Conclusion

THE WORK WITCH'S PATH TO EMPOWERMENT

As you close this book, remember that being a Work Witch is not about adding pressure to "do it all" or "have it all." It's about weaving your craft and intentions into the fabric of your professional life in natural and empowering ways. Whether your journey has just begun or you're refining practices you've held for years, know that magic is not a destination—it's a process of mindful alignment with whom you are and where you want to go.

Magic as Everyday Empowerment

The modern workplace can be demanding, but it is also an incredible canvas for creativity, intention, and self-discovery. By approaching work as a sacred space, you shift your perspective from stress and obligation to opportunity and empowerment.

- Every ritual you perform, no matter how small, declares your agency.

- Every crystal you carry, every intention you set, is a step toward shaping your energy.

- Every moment you ground yourself amidst chaos, you affirm your resilience and strength.

This journey isn't about making work "perfect" but meaningful, balanced, and sustainable.

The Power of Self-Care

Self-care is the cornerstone of the Work Witch's practice. It's a gentle yet firm reminder that your worth isn't tied to your productivity, and challenges don't diminish your magic. By prioritizing your well-being, you allow yourself to flourish—not just as a professional, but as a whole, vibrant being.

Let this book's rituals, tools, and techniques serve as your guide. Adapt, personalize, and integrate them into your life in ways that honour your unique energy and goals.

The Magic Is Already Within You

If there's one truth to carry with you, it's this: the magic you seek in your work life is already within you. Every intentional breath, every mindful action, and every boundary you set are reflections of your power. This book has given you tools to amplify that power, but the spark? That's all yours.

A Work Witch's Affirmation

As you move forward, keep this affirmation close to your heart:

I am aligned with my purpose, grounded in my power, and open to the magic of my work. I approach each day with intention and grace, knowing I can create space for success and self-care. My craft evolves with me, and my energy shapes the world around me.

Your Next Steps

The workplace, like magic, is ever-changing. The practices you've explored in these pages will grow with you as your career evolves. Continue experimenting, learning, and reflecting. Build on what resonates, release what doesn't, and trust your intuition to guide you.

Whether you're lighting a candle before a big presentation, grounding yourself after a stressful meeting, or simply carrying a crystal in your pocket, know that every mindful magic adds to something extraordinary.

So go forth, Work Witch. Infuse your work with intention, live in alignment with your energy, and let your unique magic shine. The world needs your light—especially at work.

Thank you

Thank You for Reading!

Thank you for joining me on this journey—I'm so grateful for your time and support! Your feedback means a lot to me, and hearing from readers is one of the best parts of being an author. If you enjoyed the book, I'd love it if you could take a moment to share your thoughts in a review on Amazon. Your reviews help other readers discover my work, and I appreciate every word.

If you'd like to reach out directly, feel free to contact me at Kelsey.Pearce.Grit@gmail.com. I'd be delighted to hear from you!

With heartfelt thanks,

Kelsey

Also by Kelsey Pearce

Mindful Magic Series:

Mindful Magic: A Guide to Modern Witchcraft for Mental Wellness & Self-Care   ISBN 978-1738290574

A beginners guide to magic and intention. This book takes a inclusive and accessible approach to magic encouraging anyone to build their our practice. Learn how to create your own spells or leverage the twenty-five premade spells.

Mindful Magic for The Kitchen Witch: Crafting Nourishment and Self-Care Through Recipes and Rituals   ISBN 978-1738290598

With simple recipes and practical insights, this book invites you to create meals that not only nourish the body but uplift the spirit. Perfect for beginner and seasoned kitchen witches alike, this guide brings magic to your daily rituals and helps you cultivate a kitchen that's brimming with intention, love, and powerful energy. Over thirty recipes leveraging easily accessible ingredients with magical properties included.

Mindful Magic for The Holiday Witch: A Guide to Winter Solstice, Yule Rituals, Self-Care, and Holiday Healing ISBN 978-1069149114

Transformative approach to the holiday season. Drawing on the timeless magic of Yule and witchcraft traditions, this guide empowers you to create a more meaningful, grounded, and balanced holiday experience.

Spell Crafting: Witchcraft resource that includes reference material for crystals, herbs, lunar magic, and more. ISBN 978-1738290567

Build your own Book of Shadows or Grimoire with these easy templates and reference material.

Resiliency and Gratitude Series:

Grateful Grit: Building Resilience Through Gratitude ISBN 978-1738290529

Learn how gratitude in the face of adversity can help build resilience and your growth mindset.

Happiness for the Senses: Mindful Sensory Experience: Taste, Touch, Sight, Smell, Sound ISBN 978-1738290505

Learn how to engage all of your senses to find happiness and mindfulness.

www.ingramcontent.com/pod-product-compliance
Lightning Source LLC
Chambersburg PA
CBHW060115050426
42448CB00010B/1883